No sex, please. We're Nigerians

A comic pastiche of Nigeria and Nigerians

by

ZAMWAWOSAI TARACHI

This book is dedicated to these following sources of inspiration:

(The late) Conor Cruise O'Brien

(The late) Michael Crawford, OBE.

Peter Enahoro

Michael Palin, CBE FRGS

Red Dwarf (TV series)

Benjamin Jonson

If man merely sat back and thought about his impending termination, and his terrifying insignificance and aloneness in the cosmos, he would surely go mad, or succumb to a numbing sense of futility. Why, he might ask himself, should he bother to write a great symphony, or strive to make a living, or even to love another, when he is no more than a momentary microbe on a dust mote whirling through the unimaginable immensity of space?

Stanley Kubrick, 1968. (in an interview for *Playboy*)

For

Laughs

Contents

Introduction

Prologue: A Scapegoat Nation

1. Who is the Nigerian?

2. Happy People

3. Where to, Guv?

4. Hello Hello!

5. Proudly Nigerian

6. Tour de Force

7. English is not my father's language

8. Are you politically correct?

9. Women left, Men right…

10. Follow the Signs

11. What is your Faith?

12. Home Movies

13. Fix me this

14. Protesters Union of Nigeria

15. Committee of the Whole

16. Power to the People

17. The National Question

18. The Sycophant

19. Original Big man

20. Adjutant, my adjutant

21. The Nigerian Law & Order Force

22. Courtesy as we like it

23. Sex

Epilogue: I Dream Nigeria

Postscript

Introduction

Conor Cruise O'Brien once said that Irishness is not primarily a question of birth or blood or language; it is the condition of being involved in the Irish situation, and usually of being mauled by it. O'Brien should have been a Nigerian, for although he spoke of his country, his immortal words apply to the Nigerian.

A fourth-generation Nigerian is born into a world where, from the beginning he is placed at the bank of the Serengeti River to cross, with the knowledge that amphibious reptiles lurk for the weak link. This Nigerian is quick to condemn, inveigle, forget his iPod earphone in his ears as he crosses the road, point the finger at the Senator, lament about corruption as he aligns himself with his fellow ethnic man to bring down the 'enemy', and comment on how infidelity is second only to watching Wayne Squealer Rooney on television. The paradox is that this Nigerian has patriotism up his eyes: he watches junk Nigerian films, listens to hollering Nigerian musicians who are concerned about their enemy haters, and employs Nigerian slang to fail his final examinations on purpose.

The question is: is this new Nigerian looking the wrong way, driving a high-performance car in reverse gear? Many pragmatist will confess to been seen as odd if you approach patriotism the way Conor Cruise O'Brien wanted his fellow whiskey-laden Irishmen to. Truth has become a relative, scarce commodity and the stuff of legend. Nigerians who find it marvel and then quickly return to their prevaricating ways. After seven years writing draught after draught, this writer is beginning to question himself. What follows is a documentation of what the typical Nigerian loves to make a joke about; anyone who does not follow these patterns, logic follows, cannot be Nigerian. I am cross-checking the details of my passport as I write....

The Nigerian is an enigma. You see him today like this, you see him tomorrow like that: he's friendly and mad at the same time, a father and a torturer, a scientist and a fetish. While you can point your finger in public at a lonely fellow minding his business as a Brit, or at a muscled-up 6-footer in a sports car as an American, you can't do the same for the Nigerian. He looks identifiable enough, yes. But after you get to know him describing him becomes a Herculean task. Someone asks you if you know a certain Shednayi Agher Ada, and you reply yes. The fellow then requests you describe him, and that's when a question mark will pop up over your head.

So, who is the Nigerian? The Nigerian is the most brilliant scientist in the world who is fetish and thinks every lunar or solar eclipse is the end of the world; he attends Mass in the mornings and pays homage to the local witchdoctor by night. His evenings are spent at the local radio station: the gossip centre. The Nigerian is polite when he should be rude; he's rude when he should be polite. He's patriotic enough not to recite his National Anthem while he dislikes the French so much he knows the "Marseillaise" by heart. He wants his country to be better off than it is now, and insists that foreigners come down to do this for him while he lounges. The Nigerian complains of petrol queues, but is happy in a visa queue. 'One Nigeria!' he declares to all and sundry, before moving on to enforce the wishes of his tribe against the other tribe.

On the whole, the Nigerian is a pleasant fellow. After you've met him, you won't want to leave him. His country is his oyster, and he proclaims his love for it backwards!

Bon appetite.

Prologue: A Scapegoat Nation

The one thing about Nigeria is that in spite of the many reports about it on international television many foreigners still can't point to the country on an atlas. And an even more unfortunate group of foreigners have arrived the shores of our great country disappointed not to see Charles Darwin's cousins hovering about in trees and chattering with sounds assumed to be some form of communication.

Tsch!

In this day and age every country seeks to be recognised. Such becomes the daily task of the Tourism PR department of CNN. An average day is spent entertaining customers from back-water countries liker Bangladesh, Sri Lanka, Zimbabwe, DR Congo, Colombia.

'Wait a minute,' Joe Mann begins as he scrutinises the advert application from Somalia, 'is not a war going on with the Al Shabaab group?'

The Ambassador nods.

'Then, that can only mean that you expect tourists to visit your country at the risk of been caught up…?'

The Ambassador nods again. Joe sighs.

'Look, serr, I don't wanna be rude but selling a war-torn country to tourists isn't exactly going to work,' Joe begins to explain, 'it would be unfair to the world to run this commercial'.

The Ambassador nods. Joe shakes his head. Hours later and the commercial airs. The government may be haggling with the Al Shabaab but the Ambassador is quick to announce that it is from his country that celebrities like and Iman and Nuruddin Farah have sprouted.

And the same applies to war zones like Zimbabwe and DR Congo. We hear that these are no-go zones and yet crisp pictures of landscapes of these countries are everywhere on the Internet.

God's Own Second Country bleeds violence and yet everyone (especially Nigerians) work themselves into a frenzy just to end up there.

This effort is at least seven years in the making. Part of the reason is that in its early draught I managed to contact the liaison officer of a certain publishing house in London, which will remain nameless.

'A book on Nigeria you say?' he enquired in that drab, emotionless tone Brits are notorious for.

'Yes,' I began to explain, 'it is meant to showcase Nigeria for what we truly are'.

The next line was a jab: 'And *what* are you?' I promptly checked the cell phone to make sure the contact name wasn't reading 'Martian'….

In many ways I'm grateful for that fellow. The draught would have made print, yes, but as it was – after the paradox hit me, that is – it didn't stand a chance with its evolved brother seven years later.

The paradox is that how is it possible that the Biggest Black Power south of the Sahara (we're modest not to claim it all, lest our brothers in Afric du Sud take offence), once famed for having a dark-goggled strong man at the helm who ended the Liberian civil war debacle, not be mentioned on the map? Open an atlas and you'd trace Niger, Cameroon, Benin Republic and Chad.

Where's Nigeria? In the middle, surrounded by all the others? That's the answer! The experts responsible for the atlases have placed an entry labelled 'Nigeria'; but that's where it stops. Take that same atlas to a child in Geography class and ask him to point at Nigeria on that page…he'll flip the page to the African continent and direct his finger at Algeria.

Nigeria is a scapegoat nation. When the world talks of Africa in good terms, tourism goes to Kenya, healthy economy to Afric du Sud, and intellectual heritage to Mali. And what do we get? Bird flu, high infant and maternal mortality rates, pestilence, legendary refuse dumps, corruption up your eyes…the list goes on in circles.

The politicians – our very ready frontline defence – rise to the occasion to ask, 'Why?' Nigeria, they say, is blessed with many human and natural resources. Why doesn't the foreign press pick these up? For example, our elections are film plots yet to be rivalled even by the gods at Hollywood; we have a health system last to none; our patronage of luxury and second-hand cars outweighs our supply of petrol; we run the only aerial casket service, courtesy of our planes (an added bonus ensures the aircraft remains unfound for weeks: some clients request an anonymous cremation)…and many other recourses too boundless to mention.

So, is this piece of literature a response to what the foreign press doesn't know about Nigeria? To profess in the affirmative would be to be the frontline defence – a role I can't possibly shoulder. However, I hope that by the time anyone is through with this – and I refer in majority to the foreign press – more light would have been shed on the dark nation.

1. Who is the Nigerian?

Whether you're coming into the country for the first time or you're born into a Nigerian family, it is worth knowing where you are. You may spot an American by his haughty walk and bullshit talk; a Brit is identifiable by the economy of his speech; and the Asian by the squint of his eyes. But, who is a Nigerian?

A Nigerian is not a cliché or a Universal Constant. Like a random variable identifying him requires skill, tact, humour, deceit, camaraderie and a good measure of tolerance. He is like this now and like that later.

MOTORING. You're driving down town, after your usual up-and-down. The cool evening breeze is in your face and the voice through the FM stereo jack is keeping you and your friends company. Then, as you approach a junction, a driver swerves into your way. You swerve back, avoiding him by millimetres. As you and your friends barely recover from the shock, you drop your foot on the throttle to level up with the offender to register your protest. As you get your car to his nearside you bark out: 'My friend, were you blind? Stupid fool! How can you just enter the road like that? I had the right of way; I could have easily run into you'.

If the fellow is a foreigner he'll plead, 'Apologies. I was in a bit of a rush...' and it ends there. You both hoot your horns to seal the reconciliation and life continues.

But if the offender is Nigerian he'll crank his head towards you, look through you and remark, 'Well done. Mister Traffic Warden'.

'?'

And he drops his foot on the throttle....

Another interesting feature of the Nigerian driver is the way he handles his car. Russians and Brits are notorious for having both hands on the wheels (except during gear shift) and with eyes fixed at the advance as in parade formation. Wave at a Russian and he answers when he has reached his destination... with a phone call!

The Nigerian driver is a phenomenon. From the moment he starts his car one hand rests on the window frame. He shifts gear with the hand he has on the wheel and – if installed – the same hand scans music tracks on the disc player. With the same hand he answers an incoming call as well, adjusts his rear view mirror, checks inside the glove compartment for pen and paper to copy down a few details from the caller, shift gear, change music track, disconnect the call, before finally replacing that hand on the wheel. And all this while the car has maintained its lane to the last millimetre!

****

Never attempt to fight over the road with a taxi driver. You'll end up with a battered car and he will have added just another dent on his as a trophy to his many road-carnage victories. If you spot a three-tonne articulated truck in your rear-view mirror coming at you at 100 kilometres per hour, relax and maintain your lane. Nothing is going to happen; if you spot a monochrome saloon with stripes 200 metres away cruising at 50 per hour, signal to your right and park. It is for your own good. For you may think that the distance between that taxi and your car isn't much of a worry. Wait until he spots a commuter in front of you. Then you make another check of your rear and, he isn't there again! Wossai? Then he's at your offside, raging at 100 per hour. Is he hurrying to the next town? Not in Hosanna's lifetime! He swerves into your front, missing you by millimetres, and screeches to a smooth stop seconds away (watch out for the limp left arm he has put out to signal, as an afterthought). Having been spared from sudden death you slow down to exchange altercations with the mad man. As you monologue, the taxi man is busying himself sorting things with his passenger who has just come on board. As this is Nigeria, your protest is nothing new to the driver. He maintains his ignorance and drives off, leaving you to continue your monologue

****

A true Nigerian with a penchant for motoring will fork out thousands to buy a shiny new car while he's still struggling to pay his light, water and telephone bills in a two-bedroom flat which appears more like the end-line of a shooting range than like a habitat.

It was a sunny afternoon, and, like any sensible animal, my friends and me were seated under a tree to cool off (there hadn't been power for at least five hours – and worse records usually exist). As we got to the crux of an argument a huge four-wheel drive of a car, glinting in sable and appearing more like am ocean liner on the tarmac , began to cruise by. And rue to its size it kept driving by without end, as a train would at a Railway Crossing. One of my comrades – the expert among us on all things automotive – remarked about the vehicle's price tag.

'Twelve million Naira?' I ejaculated. I must say that I thought this was pornographic. The price tag, that is.

'Yah,' Jeremy Clarkson said, with an air of pride in a trade he doesn't get paid for.

'It must be one of these big shots,' another of my friends began, 'I heard he has a whole yard full of them'.

And so the commentary continued as the proud beast paraded its splendour. When at last it did get by we followed it to see where it would end. It continued its cruise for another fifty metres before it signalled left and drove into a compound popular with Nigeria as 'Face-me-I-face-you'.

Only a Nigerian would understand the meaning of this paradox….

When you see a haggard fellow in a beat-up saloon that should belong in the National Archives, tread carefully. He is David with a sling. One phone-call from his equally derelict cell phone could get your luxury car towed to the Vehicles Inspection Office. Anybody with power on the road that doesn't appear so is a Nigerian.

BUSINESS. 'How much is this?'

Pause.

'I say how much is this?'

'Because I know you, just bring five hundred Naira'.

'Okay then. Here you are'—

If you're a trader and someone hands you the money on first contact, beat it. That fellow is a ritualist and then next time you see him he'll be paying a price for you.

Proper Nigerian business should transpire as follows:

'How much is this?'

Pause.

'I say how much is this? Or you don't want to sell it'.

'Emm, because you're my customer just bring five hundred Naira'.

(This is a lie, as this is the first time you've set eyes on this fellow or his stall)

'Haba, this thing. It's not worth five hundred'.

'Ah, Oga. It is. It's even worth seven hundred, but because I know you I decide for you to have it at fair price. Pay five hundred'.

Pause.

‘No, I can’t pay that amount. I’ll give you one hundred’.

‘One-what. Haba, Oga. Take a look at this product: it’s the real thing, genuine. Made in China. And this is the last one I have; take it while stocks last’—

‘One fifty’

‘Two hundred’

‘One seventy’

‘One eighty. Last price’.

‘One ninety. Last offer’.

Pause.

‘All right then. One ninety. But it is because I know you that I’m going to buy this at this price. Next time I’ll pay lower’.

‘Okay, Oga’….

There will be no Next-time and you both know that product was worth ninety Naira.

****

A woman was rushing across the market, beating her breast and crying the Lamentations. Her sojourn stopped at the city centre where she found Baba Iyabo, a neighbour and taxi-driver. He was seating in his race car, at the front of a taxi rank, waiting for his last passenger to come aboard.

‘Baba Iyabo, Baba Iyabo’, she cried as she got to his taxi, throwing herself on the tarmac.

Baba Iyabo, in equal drama, flew out of the taxi and onto the tarmac, crying and throwing himself about. The passengers were taken aback by the melancholia. After about a minute of the rendition, Baba Iyabo managed to enquire, ‘Mama Kemi, what is it? What is the matter?’

Mama Kemi, struggling to wipe her tears, announced to her neighbour that his father, who had come visiting from the country, had just passed on.

'What!'

The dirge resumed for another minute, and this time the taxi driver was begging to be left alone, for him to be allowed to follow his late father, threatening to throw himself in front of a moving car (it is noteworthy that no one was really holding him back from doing anything).

'Baba, please come quickly,' Mama Kemi suggested, yanking her neighbour by the hand as she led the way. But just as the passengers were going to protest on who'll drive them into town, Baba Iyabo yanked back his arm and announced, 'Mama Kemi, you go on ahead. I'll come by after dropping these passengers'. And he finished his sentence behind the wheel.

Is Baba Iyabo without concern? Not at all. He's a Nigerian. A Nigerian trader-businessman who delays his money-making venture to attend to something else is foolish; a Nigerian trader-businessman who thinks of the money day and night is clever. Don't expect any sympathy from this fellow.

GEOGRAPHY. Nigeria is a cosmopolitan expression. You enter China and it's all about squinty-eyed average citizens walking about. In Nigeria, this is not the case. You see Lebanese in Kaduna, Lebanese in Jos, Lebanese in Minna—and yet our flag has the colours green and white. For starters, how do you tell which part of Nigeria you're in?

Where are We?

The country is a vast sheet of savannah and Sahel, dust and mud, villages and cities. From above you may find it difficult to say where you are. What happens if your aero plane experiences turbulence and the Captain gives the last order – to jump. Well, you jump of course.

Upon landing, the first thing you have to do is try to identify where upon this Earth you have landed. Don't attempt to check your map, or beat your hands at animals. These tactics will fail and you will be frustrated. In the manner of a homeless tramp begin to wonder about. Your first contact will determine if you're still on this planet and where.

Your first contact is a human being. Ahh, you interject. I'm home. But this human being is like none you've seen: his head is oblong and the size of his nose suggests to you that at any moment from now the air supply around you may begin to thin out. In your idiocy as a foreigner don't ask: 'Excuse me, where am I?' This will only make *you* the alien. Act as though you've been taking a stroll. Salute him thus: 'Well done-o. How are things?'

If the fellow scratches his occipital and speaks through his nose as he answers, '*Nna* men, business is not moving well', you're sure you're somewhere in Eastern Nigeria. Move along, for that's what this fellow will paralyse you with in his conversations.

However, it is possible that during your drop there was a powerful gale and in spite of your efforts to direct the parachute the wind won. You landed in the middle of nowhere, at dusk. Dress down and take a walk. If you come across a kaftan-wearing hermit who has a transistor radio for company, don't panic. This isn't Basra and the radio isn't a home-made I.E.D[1]. Approach the fellow and salute with an open palm in mid-air. If you execute the greeting properly, the fellow will salute back, '*A sallam'u aliakum*'. Again, stay where you are. This isn't Arabic for, 'kill the infidel!' Salute back again and welcome yourself to the North.

A third possibility is that your vessel capsized somewhere on the Gulf of Bonny. After several days you drift until you come to shore. As you rise from the ocean current you spot a food joint in the distance. Currents of relief! You begin to make for the spot. But as you approach you pick up faint chattering noises. Squinting you see the woman at the joint has begun jumping about,

---

[1] Improvised Explosive Device

uttering a series of unending phrases which sound like Shaolin prayer-points. Within seconds the woman has announced to her neighbours the forbidden news, pointing in your direction. More seconds later the entire coast is deserted, leaving the shops, eateries and stalls to fend for themselves.

Odd, you remark to yourself. However, you take a look at yourself and realise you may not be in your best appearance (having swam for days you look now like John the Baptist). So, *that*'s what frightened them off? They must have thought you were a water deity. You're in the West....

==

=====

Don't be misled into thinking that the indigenes of the West are deity worshippers, Igbos are businessmen and that all Northerners are Muslims who pass time selling chewing gum by the roadside. That line of thinking is the job of the BBC. There are Northerners who are Catholics, Igbos who worship water deities, and Westerners who make avarice a joke. You should only apply the above-mentioned tactic as a last resort.

The Geo-political Expression

Mapping Nigeria requires guile and tact. If you work for the BBC Nigeria is just three places: North, West and East. If you step into Nigeria, however, you quickly discover that Nigerians aren't exactly fans of the BBC. Ask a certain Preye where he's from and he'll say Bayelsa State.

'Ahh, Southern Nigeria', you opine.

'Nooo,' he protests, 'South-South!'

And the same applies to everyone you meet. A Kaduna man in Kaduna North says he's a Northerner; his colleague just three kilometres away in Kaduna South says he's North Central. Further down in Lako (Sarkin-Pawa on the map; two hours drive south of Kaduna city) the Gbagyis are convinced they're not North Central: Middle Belt is the slogan.

Borno is registered as North East, and Kano, just a stone's throw away, is Northern-North. If you venture to venture further out you're sure to come across a Tuareg who calls his brothers (whom you've left behind by half an hour), 'infidels'.

The puzzlement of the phenomenon of the geo-political expression is a past-time by any serious Nigerian. We eat it, sleep on it, pray for it's success, attempt to destabilise it, and so on.

Whenever news that a Nigerian who is abroad is harassed by the local police filters down, Nigerians will demonstrate their solidarity thus:

SOUTHERNER: Foul! The Cosmopolitan Police has bitten more than it can chew

SOUTHERN-SOUTHERNER: Aha! Another southerner has gone and disgraced *his* people's name

EASTERNER: These southerners are not smart people. No police can touch an easterner

WESTERNER: That name mentioned on the 9 o'clock news…sounds like an easterner

EASTERNER: No way! That person is definitely from the west

WESTERNER: That's slanderous. How dare you!

MIDDLE BELTER (passing by): Look at those southerners arguing like boys with toys…

EASTERNER: Watch it, you bloody Northerner…

MIDDLE BELTER (inching closer): Who says I'm from the North… I'm Middle belt

WESTERNER: Same thing!

NORTHERNER (sliding in, out of nowhere): What's the matter?

WESTERNER: Your brother here is denying his heritage. He says he's *not* form the North

NORTHERNER (to MIDDLE BELTER, avuncular): Brother, do not speak so… we are all one

MIDDLE BELTER: Take you hands off me, infidel

NORTH-WESTERNER: Hold on, that's my line

NORTH-EASTERNER: Ha ha!

NORTH CENTRAL: You are all insane. Lets' stop all this bickering and unite for the common cause

SOUTH SOUTHERNER: Common cause my foot! With all the religious crises in the North?

NORTHERNER: Point of correction, please. Jos is in the Middle Belt

MIDDLE BELTER: No it's not. It's close to Bauchi; that makes it North Central

ALL AND SUNDRY—EXCLAMATION MARKS OVER THEIR HEADS

And the bickering continues. However, let not the stereotype acrimony fool you. There is a rare occasion when a lizard morphs into a dog to get favour from Bingo. And a typical situation is the response to a job vacancy. Let's assume that a post has been advertised to be vacant and the man at the helm of the agency is a Muslim from Kano state. An applicant from Niger State approaches him. If both are co-religionists then the applicant is guaranteed a job because he is a 'brother'. However, if another applicant from the same state is *not* of the same religion with the Service provider the Niger-lite can kiss his application letter goodbye. His crime: he's from the Middle Belt.

2. Happy People

In the 2003, the International Committee of Western Scientists congregated in London – the global capital of Cockney Jews – and after a session that lasted weeks of tea and strenuous investigation they came to the conclusion that Nigerians were the happiest people on God's earth. Nigerians rejoiced. At last, they heaved, something good could come out of the West: none of that reporting by the BBC and the CNN who paid for refuse bins to be planted here and there and then run a feature on 'dirty Nigeria'. The ICWS had made Nigeria's day.

Much later, the Committee published the criteria which assisted them in their findings. They are as follows:

(Abridged version)

a) A Nigerian who gets knocked down by a speeding car just millimetres from an over-head bridge is said to be happy

b) When PHCN – the power supply company – cuts power for weeks on end, the Nigerian lives the ordeal like all is well

c) The Government decides to increase pump price of fuel and Nigerians harangue themselves. The following day they don't embark on a strike. They embark on a Compliance spree to adapt to the new price. This is a sign of happiness in the government

In addition to the above the ICWS also discovered – as did Mungo Park to River Niger – the singular thing that keeps Nigerians going: the Act of the God Paradox.

The Act of God Paradox is the ultimate excuse in surrender, the avenue by which Nigerians remember there is a God.

When a motorcycle runs over a child in broad daylight in spite of the over-head bridge just metres away, passers- and standers-by will go irate. They may even incinerate the poor driver. But, after all has been said and done we gather around and proclaim, 'it is an act of God' in consolation. Nobody thinks of having to campaign for the publicity of the over-head bridge; or even for the Road Safety Authorities to erect a speed limit sign close by. And so, children will continue to jay walk across the road, and drivers will continue to throttle at top speed when they do. This is because Nigerians believe that everything is an act of God.

And thus we drive without buckling up, less crash helmets, self-medicate when ill (and in some cases leave all to the Almighty), and so on. The notion is that God is in charge of all – no human effort ever contributes or success or mishaps. And so we live our lives 'waiting for God's time' every time.

***Play it Again, Oga*[1]**

If you wish to humour the Nigerian give him a record. For as long as he has this everyone else can go blazes – to the Arctic. When I was growing up it was common for the foreign press to report Nigeria in bad light. Now, they know better: they now report Nigeria in darkness. The foreign press – itself the guard-dog to the ICWS – is notorious for humouring Nigerians. They say we are the most corrupt, the poorest of the poor, the wealthiest, the most football fanatic, and so on. This reporting is clearly stereotyped and, if I may interject, does not belong to twenty-first century Nigeria. If any member of the foreign press wishes to report the millennium us then there are a few up-to-date records that are noteworthy:

---

[1] Colloquial, 'boss' or anyone considered a superior. Sometimes employed as a humour gimmick

A Nigerian is the happiest man in the world when he walks – sorry, strays – into the road and gets knocked down by a car in spite of the over-head bridge less than a metre away;

Abuja is on record as been the fastest growing city in the world – when others have finished growing!

A Governor commissions an institute in his state and proclaims it, 'The first of its kind south of the Sahara'. This is because every other country south of the Sahara doesn't really need that type of institute, hence the elimination of competition;

We're the largest black nation in the world – the headquarters of the Black Simians' Movement is in Harlem;

We were the first country south of the Sahara to report a case of avian influenza; we were also the first country to anticipate the possible outbreak of its successor, swine flu.

As I write there is pandemonium at Beijing Airport. A Nigerian is the only one wise enough to jump through a glass window and land four floors down. Other Africans patrons present stood by and watched him set and smash a record – and a pane of glass. Pun unintended.

3. Where to, Guv?

One of the ways to acquaint oneself with places in Nigeria is to be a Johnny Just Come*: you have to be lost! And when you're lost, you ask for directions; these directions will then lead you out of your peril and into more lost-ness (pardon the neologism).

But first, a word or two from our sponsors…sorry, a word or two about being lost.

In a modern city with just about every essential facility in good working condition, been a Johnny Just Come is no big deal. You can take the whole day savouring your new environment, ogling school girls, window shopping, and any other trivial triviality. Then your watch tells you it's getting late, and you have to find a place rather quickly. Looking around you notice a good citizen whom you might ask directions. This person is usually the Devil's workshop, idling around in one place so that he appears to be scheming to steal a vagrant's meal. Approaching the fellow, you make yourself known to him as a mark of friendship. He reciprocates as though sampling you as his next victim (his wide grin is already giving him away).

"Please, how do I get to Mungo Park Avenue?" you enquire.

The fellow works like a dragon fly on steroids. His reply comes like the movements of a robot.

"O, that's easy," he remarks, as though you could just fly there without a moment's notice. But he's still talking. "From here, go down the road, turn to the first right into Colonial Street, and hail a cab. From there it's a five-minute drive".

Relieved beyond joy you decide to reward the fellow with a tip. Much to your surprise, and in sharp contrast to which he seemed a while ago, he turns down your proffer of gratitude. You insist, and he desists. And with that you both part ways as though something quicker than a quickie has just transpired. Anyway, seven minutes later, you're at Mungo Park Avenue….

From here on you have to establish which accommodation will serve well at an affordable board rate. Again, a good citizen is at hand. Briskly she gives you directions with the deft movement of

* Vernacular slang, "newbie", better known by its abbreviated form J.J.C

her lips before she continues her scuttle. In no time you locate your hired abode of choice and the evening continues like a path on a map. Easy as ABC.

Now you're in Nigeria. You're a Johnny Just Come and you naturally have to ask for directions to St Gerald's Catholic Church, your new posting. You're in your air-conditioned car and park at the kerb to enquire from a well-dressed gentleman.

'Excuse me, how do I get to St Gerald's?'

You notice when you stopped the fellow beamed. This should not be mistaken for eagerness of hospitality. It is a clear sign the fellow wouldn't mind a lift in your air-conditioned car! So, as you as you ask for directions his face drops to something of a scowl of disappointment.

'St Gerald's?' he quizzes himself, scratching at his occipital. It seems to him you have mentioned a non-existent planet. He continues the quizzing, 'St Gerald's...St Gerald's...St Gerald's...'. After two days, he snaps and you light up a bit with relief.

'Kai, oga. I don't know where that is,' he announces, his hand still behind his head. Just as you give up he snaps again, 'but you can ask that man there'. He points at another citizen. You thank him for nothing and alight from your car to get to 'dat man'. You get to that man, extend your hands to proffer acquaintance and then put forward your request. That man snaps like the other man, 'Okayyy,' he interjects, one finger in his on the bridge of his lips as he jugs his memory, 'Sent Gerahddi!' And like the other fellow he repeats the name over and over like a mantra to make something click. At this point you collapse inside, helpless. In fact you have begun looking around for a policeman, the first person you should have acquainted for directions. Just as you find one a few metres away this fellow places a hand on your shoulder. He has good news.

'See, ba,' he begins, 'when you reach *that* (his finger a waving dial) junction you'll enter. Then the second road you see, enter that wan. As you enter just go straaaaaaight. You go see the signboard of Sent Gerahd'. The direction he's given seems vague but you thank him all the same. But just as you get back into your car you remember that when he pointed at that junction you saw two. Strange? Well, you're in Nigeria. And here finding your way is no different than a game of poker. So, you throw your dice and drive to that junction. Sorry, those junctions....You get there and take your chances. You're done making enquiries. You turn at the first junction and lo and behold *is* Saint Gerald's. Didn't the ingrate say go straight?

When asking for directions be prepared to spend the entire day getting to your destination which may be a stone's through away. A typical Nigerian description goes thus:

'You see that road? Right. Now head straight for it. You'll see a junction, okay? Don't turn there. Instead turn at the next junction. Keep going straight until you see a big blue building. That's not where you're going. Ignore it and proceed left, okay? Keep going straight until you see a house with green roof at the end. That's not your destination. Rather, look right and you'll see where it is you're headed…'. If you follow these direction strictly you're bound to pop out at a dusty road with a dead-pan sign reading WELCOME TO CHAD REPUBLIC!

4. Hello…

Before the G.S.M revolution (pre-1999):

CALLER: Hello, Godwin. How far?

RECEIVER: Fine-o, my brother.

CALLER: How is the family?

RECEIVER: They are fine. And your own? How are they all?

CALLER: They are fine. We thank God. How are the children?

RECEIVER: They are fine. And your own, how are they?

CALLER: They are fine. One of them has just started college.

RECEIVER: Ahh, das very good. Simi is it? She is now a big girl

CALLER: Yes. We give God the glory. So, how is everything? How is work?

RECEIVER: Well, we're patching up here and there, trying to manage.

CALLER: My brotha, das how things are in this country-o; it is just to manage. Where there is life there is hope.

RECEIVER: Mm.

PAUSE

RECEIVER: So, how is everything?

CALLER: Fine

RECEIVER: And how is that refuse in front of your house. Did you manage to get to the Urban Development people to come and clear the ordure?

CALLER: Ah, don't mind those damned civil servants! They are waiting for me to grease their palm.

RECEIVER: Again? When will this country change, henh? For somebody to come and do his job he wants a bribe—?

CALLER: Ach! Don't talk like you're not a Nigerian. Any way, how is your car? The other day I passed you by at the mechanic shed—

RECEIVER: Ah, that car. I almost regret buying it sef. Imagine! From one problem to the other. Today it's the kick starter, tomorrow the fuel pump gives up, the next time it is another thing—

DIALOGUE CONTINUES FOR ANOTHER TWO DAYS

During the G.S.M Revolution (between 1999 and 2003):

CALLER: Hello

RECEIVER: Hello

CALLER: Hello, hello... can you hear me?

RECEIVER: Hello, are you there?

CALL ENDED TONE

REDIAL

CALLER: Hello

RECEIVER: Yes, hello

CALLER: Aha, what happened?

RECEIVER: To what?

CALLER: I called awhile ago and it seemed you didn't want to answer

RECEIVER: No, not at all. I did answer. But—

FEMALE COMPUTER-VOICE: Your call credit has been exhausted and your call terminated! Please load a recharge to avoid service suspension.

After the G.S.M Revolution (2005 upwards):

CALLER: Hello. How far? Please come over to my place. There's a lot to discuss on that issue

CALL ENDED TONE

RECEIVER (into dead end): Okay.

Nigerians were once notorious for been social, especially with conversation. Alas, democracy was restored in 1999 and with it came the G.S.M revolution. Nigerians, still hung from the hang-over of the NITEL[1] days, tried to fit in their lust for long talk into their portable cell phones. But the imperialist companies would not have it, and since then Nigerians have become talk-zombies. When your call credit runs out, what do you do? Remember an old friend who owes you one. Buzz. If that friend is what the salt he or she will call back, at which you must humble yourself and ask for a certain amount of credit. It is usually easier if you're a girl enamored to some pot-bellied Senator who is under the assumption you love him more than his wallet. For the male folk,

[1] Nigerian Telecommunications Commission, telecoms landline operator

if you run out of talk credit, grind ashes, spray on your head and wrap yourself with sack-cloth…your problems have just begun.

5. Proudly Nigerian

Any Nigerian who is proud of the flag is a raging bull on the loose, a vagabond out to cause Grievous Bodily Harm. Never get in the way. A Nigerian who loves his country won't settle for second place anywhere.

When a Nigerian tells you his country is the giant of Africa just admit it; argue that Nigeria's influence has waned in the last decade and you could make the Crucifixion a joke!

When a Nigerian says his Army is the best on the Continent just agree, knowing fully well that the Army operates a 1940s approach to war.

The slang 'Proudly Nigerian' has conveniently replaced the National Anthem…and many people still don't know this.

Observe that whenever the National Anthem is played citizens stay rigged in their seats; and then when a local sub-standard product is released into the market the same people chant, 'proudly Nigerian!'

The slogan is an avenue for patriots to celebrate mediocrity and to deny the obvious truth. It sounds like something we picked up from the South Africans, but it has been with us from the 1990s. I recall how I found out the hard way what it means to be proudly Nigeria. It was World Cup 1998 and the Nigerian team was struggling with a slim chance to the Final 16. The Super Eagles were to play the Danish and that day I prophesied that, given our previous performance at the qualifying stage, the Eagles did not stand a chance of going through the Danes. In fact, I went on to say that the score line would be five goals to four in favour of the opponent. I was in Junior Secondary then. Like my role model, a *fatwa* was declared on me. I went into hiding, having survived the first wave of persecution. It turned out, however, that *we* (notice the compulsion of acceptance) lost the match 1—5.

Our distinguished parliamentarians are proudly Nigerian. They stand up from their comfy seats – manufactured by German hands – and proclaim to all and sundry that patronising Made-in-Nigeria goods is the surest way to development. After debating, they are chauffeured in their luxury sedans to the nearest shopping mall to buy Italian shoes, Swiss watches, Malian tailoring, French toothbrushes, etc. For their wives – or girlfriends – they get to enjoy been patriotic by doing their shopping in Paris or Dubai. These same females return with Faberge jewellery and tell their less-fortunate colleagues that it is good to patronise home-made goods. After all, they opine, 'we have no other country to call our own'.

If you happen to be in a fuel queue and you notice somebody trying to queue barge, approach him for a little drama. You put it to him that what he's about to do is not quite correct. The fellow, if he's proudly Nigerian, will respond thus, a hand on your shoulder, 'Anh-anh, my *broda*. You're behaving as if you're not a Nigerian…'. It then dawns on you that *you* might *actually* be a foreigner with your philosophy about discipline and morality. After all, the fellow is a proud Nigerian – this you can tell by the lapel pin of the green and white map of Nigeria he has pinned to his tunic.

N.B

To be proudly Nigerian is for the elite of the elite, second only to trained fighter pilots. The first thing you require to be a proud Nigerian is high taste. Nothing Nigerian should be able to quench your lust for high living, down to bottled water. At the same time you need to keep the teeming masses behind the lines by constantly preaching patronage of home-made goods (home-made goods, mind you, are devoid of warranty and are the perfect example of half-life).

A proud Nigerian must be a smart fellow (in local colloquialism we say 'sharp'). This means you're constantly on the look-out for the slightest opportunity for the easy way out of anything:

you should be able to join a 51-vehicle-long petrol queue as the fifty-second car and suddenly appear as the third car in line before anyone can scream Sani Abacha; you should be able to circumvent protocol by greasing palms, while your faithful compatriots stand clueless under the sun.

Finally, the identity. Aside your mouth you should be able to be identified from a distance. You should have he infamous green and white map of Nigerian insignia pinned to your lapel.

That done you are now a certified proud Nigerian.

6. Tour de force

Tourism is the new market of the 21st century. Everybody is doing it. Even small-wigs like Bangladesh with as little as police batons putting protesters in order has an ambitious tourism programme to lure foreign currency in. Tourism isn't about white men and women polluting your beaches in bikinis and night-time orgies; it's about putting your country on the map. Think Thailand with swarms of westerners patronising brothels and lolitas. You may occupy a large land mass in the geographic scale of things, but if someone elsewhere on the globe doesn't know your country by heart then you haven't started.

However, lest we be deceived by the definition of tourism, the flashy home videos shown of other countries on CNN is *not* tourism. Tourism has to come with curiosity, a longing to commit the abominable sin by sneaking in and out of a hotspot and then reporting the news to alarmed and impressed neighbours and friends.

'I was in Cuba last week,' you narrate to your audience.

'Issalie!' protests one.

'Didn't the Communist Police arrest you?' puts in another.... And the debate goes on, with you playing the adventurer who has found his way back to civilisation.

Tourism is the business of idle white men and women, armed with cameras, engaging themselves in the shanty areas of your country and e-mailing the pictures back to friends and families back home. Finish. For one therefore to attract these idle white men and their thirst for international gossip you don't have to be Truly Asian; which is where a handy suggestion comes in: the Zimbabwe Paradox.

The mention of Zimbabwe immediately generates a mental picture of a former warlord cum strongman cum Herod who presides over a nation riddled with reverse discrimination, cholera and a currency rate that has become the stuff of legend. Thanks to all this Zimbabwe is on the map. Forget what the international community says; they always have *something* to say anyway.

If Nigeria wishes to be on the map then adapting the Zimbabwe Paradox is a good option. Of course, we don't have a madman as Head of State – we've had several! – and our currency isn't on its way to the Guinness Book of Records; but there is a way all the same: curiosity.

Any idle white man and/or his wife lounging in their apartment need to be spurred to want to risk begging from their neighbours and relatives to travel down to Nigeria.

a) CONTRACT. Many tourists and foreign investors (as our journalists would call them) love a good contract, because many of them are actually CIA-trained federal lobbyists out to chart uncharted territory and plant the country's flag in as little a space as possible.

Nigeria should put an offer to bidders to purchase its most valuable resource, which could be anything, really. The amount on offer should be pornographic. Westerners can't resist this one.

The offer also has to be periodic – the white man is not known to settle down. He carts away the loot to his country to be taxed.

Meanwhile, have a financial crimes officer on standby ready to arrange for tax evasion in the form of bribes worth twelve times the tax. This sort of intrigue is sure to make the white man trace Nigeria on the map…with carbon paper!

b) CULTURAL FESTIVAL. A nation shows itself by dance and drumming. We should have a carnival, but not the vein of Caranval del Rio or Nothing Hill. That is a different kettle. The Nigerian Cultural Festival should be ludicrous to the point of pity.

Sacred masquerades, previously unseen even to some clan elders, should be allowed to parade themselves in public; the cameras should be there as well to capture the unmasked taboos.

The dancers – majority of them should be nubiles – should be clad in Nigerian attire(, with material thin enough to emphasise the generosity of the hindquarters. They must be instructed to wiggles their behinds as they file past tourists. The hotels will be waiting later in the evening….

c) ELECTION. Idle tourists are inseparable from African elections. However, other countries are have become so civil in the election business that monitoring no longer becomes necessary. And so over time westerners can just sit back and tune the BBC to watch elections in Ghana, Namibia and so on, go on without threat of disturbance to western interests.

Even as Nigeria continues to fool itself that it is the Biggest Black Power south of the Sahara, it is pertinent that the Government stalls the perfection of elections. This is good excuse for tourists to swoop time every election year... not to observe, but to watch over western economic interests which might be jeopardised by election violence.

The election violence itself should be an issue for detectives in Scotland Yard. To the untrained ear, it is the clash of rival parties. To the trained camera it is the fallout of an age-old dispute mired by rival religions who occupy the same territory and who by curious quirk of fate split into rival political parties. If this is executed properly, with the Government playing Big Brother at the last minute and issuing press statements about how safe and peaceful the country is, then the country is sure to become a black dot in any atlas.

7. English is not my Father's Language...

* see Epilogue: I Dream Nigeria

As a foreigner, you may be taken aback when you hear a Nigerian proclaim, especially inside of an argument, 'Well, English is not my father's language...!' The situation is made all the more mysterious because the Nigerian has registered his protest in the very language he claims not to be an expert in. Is this some sort of gimmick? Hardly. In fact, not at all. When the Nigerian says English is not his mother tongue and that he should not be blamed for laughable errors in his speech, he's damned serious.

The enigma of the English language in Nigeria has had scholars banging heads against walls for decades now. Some have given up all together; others are still convinced that light at the end of a tunnel where all mining activities have ceased for years....

English language was the one thing the British had to forget. They dehoisted the Union Jack, combed home Lord Lugard's property, withdrew from Provincial Offices, and even stowed away the original recipe for tea (which is why Nigerians still think the chocolate beverage they consume in sub-zero temperature is 'tea'). But the English language had to be left off the carriage, and cleverly too.

It is standard operating procedure for Her Majesty's loyal terriers to always forget an item in an erstwhile colony which is sure to act object of discord. Remember the Coca-Cola bottle from the first instalment of *The Gods Must Be Crazy*? Well, English in Nigeria has been *that* bottle....

Don't get the wrong picture, though. The Nigerian is not smashing his neighbour with bottles because of misunderstandings...at least not yet! But there is a raft of drama goings-on which, if neglected, could warrant our rulers...sorry, leaders to begin pronouncing NIGERIA backwards!

The first time it became apparent to me that the English language was slowing the country down was during an evening walk along the dormitory escalade with a comrade of mine. We eventually veered off the campus grounds whereupon we came across an infamous sign directing attention to a barber's. At first, my comrade and I made to bolt out of the scene to the nearest police station, not to report a breach of order, but to declare ourselves missing! The sign had made it seem we had lost our way and had trespassed into cannibal territory. It read:

HEAD CUTTER...

and mercilessly continued in its sub-caption

COME FOR YOUR HEAD CUT

After about a week of self-exile, my comrade and I mustered the faith of a mustard seed and tried to move a mountain. Keeping our distance, we put it to the barber-in-charge that his signboard was rather misleading and that it was likely to scare potential patrons from his stall. We said this with half our backs turned to him (in case his signboard was dreadfully correct). He laughed haughtily, his weapon, er, tool in one hand.

'*Na today I start to dey barb head*?' he quizzed rhetorically. We said we didn't know. He proceeded to acquaint us with certain facts about how the words of his sign post did not affect the level of patronage to his stall. He talked long and hard, and eventually we began to give him our front. He summed up his defence in the famous line which Nigerians so love to use as an excuse: 'English is not my father's language...!' In that line he told us to piss off! If we had any grudges with his sign post, he suggested, it was because we were too smart!

The Nigerian likes to murder English. He resents it that much. Yet, while he's at liberty to employ native language or *patois*, he wickedly insists on using it.

Some may argue that English is the nation's single uniting factor. I beg to differ. No, I should be allowed to differ. Once upon a case, two union workers, a bus driver and his conductor, suddenly had a blow-out during a run-around. The driver, after uttering a series of curse words, called out to his comrade, 'Yackson, get down and fetch the yack so we can append the spare tyre'. Suddenly, as if seized by a violent convulsion, the conductor, Jackson, dropped off his post to the ground ejaculating copious shots of laughter. The driver, getting further irritated attempted to eviscerate what it was that had caused his round of laughter from his comrade. Surely it wasn't the flat tyre situation?

'Yackson, why are you laughing', he enquired in vernacular. The conductor was still convulsing with laughter when he managed to point a finger at the driver and uttered in spasms, '*You talk say make I go bring* "yack"; *who tell you say na* yack...*you suppose to callam* "zack"!'

Uniting factor? Tell that to the Royal Marines!

Because of the emissary of discord that is Her Majesty's Imperial Tongue, Nigerians, once obedient citizens in their various kingdoms, have been reduced to nonchalant zombies. How else would you explain a situation where a public area fertilised with enough urine to generate WMDs has the warning DON'T URINATE HERE. BY ORDER over it? Before the British brought his shenanigans, Nigerian law enforcers had their way of doing things. I've seen this apply on a rare occasion behind my dormitory room. The warning there, inscribed by a veteran of a hostel officer, read: PLEASE URINATE HERE. YOUR URINE IS NEEDED FOR RITUALS. If you visit this location even now, it is primmer than the water closets at State House.

We may not see it now, but the way out of this charade is 'Nigerianism'. That's right, the *Nigerian* way of saying things. Remember the scholars still banging their heads? Well, they don't agree. They are of the opinion that the adoption of peculiarly Nigerian expressions will lead to an abuse of standards. The poor things. The Jamaican speaks anything close to a standard form of English and he gets celebrated for it. The Nigerian converses in Nigerian and along comes a brother in Mongo Park-era suit to declare, "Your English is incorrect and fails to conform to standards...". The owner of the so-called standard, meanwhile, is busying himself, not with standards, but with a footie match coming up inside the hour.

I mean, won't it seem perfectly appropriate to have a Nigerian dictionary, for example, clearing up certain issues with foreign expressions. Why should I say, "Piss off" when "Knack out" makes more sense. I mean, imagine telling a true Nigerian to "piss off" and he'd most certainly urinate while *offing* his clothes...if he's stupid enough to understand you in the first place, that is!

Why should a hangout of distinguished uniformed men be called a "mess" when the sole purpose of patronising the place is not to mess-up the air? "Officer's Joint" should be the proper address.

For now, it seems, we can only watch everyday dramas which transpire as a result of this language discord. The country is gradually becoming like the ship in a story where the Flag Officer harangued his crew and ordered that all hands must be on deck. The day the ship was set for sail, the crewmen all stubbornly refused to take their hands off deck. The ship has not sailed till today....

8. Are You Politically Correct?

Check yourself. Are you politically correct? When you're politically correct you hold back the ordure that has accumulated over time in your bowels and instead release a fine spray of scented perfume through your rectum, enough to last while the recipient is about. To be politically correct involves tact and guile. It's not textbook philosophy; it's saving your skin and the skins of your kinsmen from certain or uncertain doom from the other party. This sort of diplomacy is usually exhibited in front of a journalist or anyone armed with mike and cam.

Let's say there hasn't been water supply in your local area for weeks on end – which isn't a strange thing in this country, really – and every morning you and your family get up as early as 3 a.m to scout for water for miles on end. After a few weeks the local TV station comes to the rescue, armed with mike, cam and questions. You're the first to benefit from their generosity.

'Sah', the half-wit journalist begins, 'how has been the water situation in your area?'

Pause. What is on your mind is that the water situation is a compete disregard for human rights, and that the perpetuators of this violation should be brought to book. You mean to say that the country has failed the Lower Class, and you are of the strong advocate for the impeachment of the Governor of your state….

'Well,' you begin, scratching your occipital in a gesture of submission, 'the situation is bad. We're suffering. For many days now we don't have water. So, what do we do? We have to get up in the morning and go and look for water…'. You pause here as the reporter returns the mike to her side.

'So, what do you want the government to do?'

She knows what the government should do; she just wants to put you in trouble. Again, you heat up. Your resolve to have the government overthrown by violent means is stronger….

'Well,' and at this you put up a facial gesture that makes even a supplicant dog look like it was acting, 'we want the government to come to our aid. We're begging them to give us water'….

If you communicate the opposite of what you really think, especially when you ought to exercise your right of speech, then you're politically correct. This does not show you're weak; it only implies you're afraid of Land Rovers loaded with government agents parking in front of your house… which is a good judge of wisdom.

Nigerians have learnt that democracy is a good thing. It helps you say one thing when you mean the opposite. This is isn't doublethink. When at a beer parlour feel free to insult the next man. Register your disgust for that person's ethnic group, whom you think are a conglomerate of lecherous vagabonds who enjoy suppressing their neighbours. The next man, if he so wishes, will return the favour. In most circumstances this may result in full-scale inter-tribal war.

Days later, after tempers have cooled and it is safe for the news crew to skulk into the ravages, when interviewed choose your words carefully. Admit that the aftermath of the argument was unjustifiable and that *that* ethnic group (whom you threw the first salvo at) are a notorious peace-loving people who wouldn't hurt a fly; the other party likewise will admit that the reaction was not from one of their number and that they too are known to be practicing pacifists. Verbal handshakes are exchanged and the news crew returns to file their story. The following week another clash between the rival ethnic groups is reported again….

Been politically correct is as delicate as striking a match in the dark with a drum of petrol millimetres away. If you think in your heart of hearts that Nupe people are second only to swine, be sure to look into a Nupe man's eyes and admit, point-blank range, that you think Nupe people are the most hard-working people in the Middle Belt. If the Nupe man is schooled in the art, he will see through your diplomacy and reciprocate by showering encomiums on *your* ethnic group. But as soon as your backs are turned the fellow directs all manner of expletives at your ethnic group, who he thinks are a band of twentieth-century barbarians.

When the authorities announce to all and sundry that the country has thirty days supply of fuel, they are been politically correct. If you are wise, get into your car and make for the nearest petrol station. If you're lucky you'd be the fifty-first car in line…!

9. Women's rights, Men's left…Everyone to the centre!

The battle between the sexes is millennia old. And the result of this battle has been the fight for women equality, the chance and right to stand shoulder to shoulder with men in all affairs. This fight has met with ups and downs, often with the men folk causing dispute among the ranks on whether women should be allotted positions of power or whether they should slug it out like everyone else. The haggling continues till this day, albeit in dissenting tones....

After decades of grumbling (this they did while icons like Rosa Parks and Billie Jean King just acted) the Nigerian woman has never had it so good. In a stretch of two terms after democracy was restored at the turn of the century women have been allotted (again they waited to be allotted) more strategic positions than at any one time in the country's history. And it's not just public servants; the mass media, entertainment, high class escort services...all sectors were affected by the revolution. And like a good dog, women leaders are still jostling for more recognition. Or is it waiting to be allotted...?

But to understand the drive towards women equality we must understand that crusader who preaches what she doesn't practice: the feminist. Yes, there is an icon. Throughout the ages women have demonstrated their zeal to be considered equal to men. From Jezebel to Delilah, Cleopatra and Marilyn Monroe, the face of the feminist has changed to suit and adapt through time and tactic.

In Nigeria, the feminist movement has adopted a curiously distinct method of advocating for female equality: segregation. Any bored follower of NTA News will recognise the plethora of fraternities (or rather, maternities) which champion women's rights across professions: the NATIONAL ASSOCIATION OF WOMEN LAWYERS; SOCIETY OF WOMEN SOCIOLOGISTS; NIGERIAN COUNCIL FOR WOMEN MEDIA PRACTITIONERS...*et cetera* and *et cetera*. As the names of these societies suggest women professionals are distinct from their male colleagues: in the profession of lawyers, for example, a woman performs segregated duties from the man even of both wear the same devil black uniform, 19th-century wigs and carry a lexicon of gibberish in their heads, the law of feminist segregation says, "*niert*!" And to some extent this tactic has worked, slowing down the recognition of women as professional equals and giving them a sort of aloof persona, a cult of Sapphics inhabiting the island of Lesbos.

If you're pitying the womenfolk you had better get over yourself: they aren't particularly worried about this paradox! Indeed they are under the notion that things are moving their way... it would be wise not to argue in the opposite!

While the term "weaker sex" has been all but abolished from public speech, the phenomenon refuses to go away because the league of feminists are employing it to their advantage. In political circles it is common knowledge that concerning positions in parliament and party hierarchy women are not known to slug it out like everyone else. Not at all! Rather, when they deem fit and set they constitute a conference of women leaders at the end of which a communiqué is issued. This paper, among other trivialities, states... no, that's not quite like it... *demands* that a certain number of seats be allotted to women politicians, to the percentage of ratio 5:4, the latter figure been theirs. To the untrained and casual eye, this demand may seem far fetched. But alas the women leaders *will* use their *boudoir repertoire* as a negotiating tool.... The following week, the demands will be met. No sweat? You can wager that.

In the animal world, the black widow, the female hyena, the lioness, the Anopheles, the termite queen and the mantis are exemplars of anything but the weaker sex; in Nigerian politics, the feminist *is* the weaker sex... just don't say it in public though, remember?

Conforming to the feminist ideology means a lot to the discerning man. It has made Nigerian men – those who bother, that is – become sensitive, limey gentlemen. The code of the gentleman demands you be gentle with your wife who knows her rights from her leftovers. If perchance you are informed by a nosy friend that your heartthrob may be having an illicit affair with some Big

Man the code demands that you head to Jos, purchase a .22-guage shotgun…and shoot your friend! As a gentleman you ought to know that your wife has her cravings and is so obliged to, em, quench them as she so wishes. Your friend, had he been a gentleman, would have lived longer….

The code further states you have to possess a battered car with the front passenger door malfunctioned. This provides a good excuse for you to attend to your wife every time you stop. Usually, an impatient passenger would just reach out the cranked down window and at the door handle; so remember to have one of those electric power windows with the controls on *your* side.

The Code is long and quite easy to follow. For details, please contact a certain airline Captain Matthew Ekeinde…he's attached to a certain actress who knows her rights from her leftovers.

Being a feminist is not quite as easy as may have been perceived from the ranting of this writer thus far. It takes the patience of a stockholder and the resilience of a pursuing cheetah. For persons who wish to go down this path, here's a walkthrough:

Start early. At 14 you should have known what it means to dress to kill. Do just that, especially with a cousin-brother to your mother's sister squatting in your father's abode. As you're dressed to kill this relative will *unsling* on you. Do not panic. Save the child for later….

Meanwhile, you're off to the University. Don't forget, though, you're now a certified man-hater, androgynous to the bone. In spite of that remember that men should know your statistics offhand. Revealing V-lines and hip huggers worn at the demilitarised zone are sure to knock eyeballs in. Your eyeliners should blind from a distance. As a hardliner you should memorise at least a one-liner (MEN CONTROL THE WORLD, WOMEN CONTROL THE MEN…for example). Rant on about how selfish men are, how the world would be a better place with women at the helm. Then at night consummate your arguments by having Big Men service you for a few wads of crispy Naira notes.

'Following thus far? Ahh. Progress.

Five years on and you've left the University behind you. From here on you're a new woman. And your lifestyle should reflect this maturity. Ditch the investment on your hair. Low cuts should be the trademark from here on, along with incongruous stockings. The revealing costumes also have to go (sorry) and in their place will be safari suits. This makes you a boy in a girls' room. Remember the kid from *that* time? Ah-hah! Bring him to the fore, your investments will yield some fruit now. The kid will be your excuse (or reason) for men not starting what they cannot finish…or is finish what they started…? No matter, you're now a certified single mother with a man-hating tongue which you'll pass on to your kid who will conveniently grow up to a mal-formed nuisance to society with twisted ideas in his head. Meanwhile in the present you are still a feminist, remember? Let the future worry about itself. You have a crusade against men to fight. The mass media should be your number one ally. Fraternise with the boss of a major television station (really, we have just *one*…). Make him at ease while you maintain a stone cold countenance and respond to his jokes with the terseness of a stiff Brit. After awhile you're sure to get the spotlight. Use it wisely. If you're allotted a 30-minute prime time slot christen your programme something catchy. "Tomorrow's Woman" should do. Or you could try "Next Afternoon With Funmi Eyonder". And on this programme remember to always pick out women under-achievers from under the noses of their male bosses. That means where you have a male boss who's the initiator of a certain public-oriented scheme, ignore him and pick the woman who heads the reception in that same organisation! With this gesture every time you're sure to be a winner with you folk any where you go.

From here you will achieve local stardom. Which implies you're now a role model. Ditch the office ware (again?) and replace with outlandish costumes like you're on your way to a Star Wars audition. Slim down massively until you're constantly mistaken for a Massai-Mara, emphasising that thin is cool while earnestly waiting for the next meal. The meals themselves should be sparsely feminist, eaten as a cat nibbles on a meal.

PAUSE. There's another option at this stage of the feminist crusade. If you however end up been a woman leader in a political party then the tactic may vary slightly. You *will* require security at this stage and that can be found by allowing an unfortunate fellow address you as his wife while you carry out your shenanigans. Here you don't tongue lash like that other feminist. It can't work here. Rather, you'll use *that* weapon of choice to grease your way up the ladder. Fraternise with your male comrades at any and every occasion, even at events as boring as party conventions. At these events dress to kill. In the dead of night – on top of your Dubai-imported chador and head-scarf – be sure to keep your sun shades on. Decorate yourself with cosmetic accessories so that you pay more attention to yourself than to your husbands phone calls about what he'll cook for the hungry kids back home.

As a Madam you have to champion your cause by asking for seats to be allotted to women and for women to come out *en masse* and join the political train. Meanwhile you content yourself with cash bonuses and anything but an allotted seat in parliament….

==

When in Nigeria the one danger of incurring the wrath of the League of Feminists is to use the wrong words at the right places.

In social gathering – a lunching for example – if a woman is presiding over ceremonies be sure to use 'chairperson' if you wish to address her properly. This implies she is just as capable of 'chair*ing*' an occasion as her male 'chairman' counterpart; and a use of the suffix –woman would imply she's distinct from men when all she wants is to be equal.

However, our chairwoman…sorry, chair*person* may be, among other things, a generous philanthropist to religious affairs. Be sure to call her a 'benefactress'. You're not been insensitive: it's a way of respecting her philanthropy, which she wishes to consider different from that of a man!

The future of feminism in Nigeria is bright. In a decade from now we'll have aeroplan*ettes* woman*ed* by pilotresses flying the across the country.

Non sequitor.

10. Follow the signs…

It is the stuff of legends that walking along a Nigerian road is a as tasking as navigating your way through a maze. Because the government wishes to be among the top 20 by 2020, it has become imperative that finding your way around will be as interesting as the 2020 vision itself. If you must understand this country, then, gents, take a walk.

At the market place (and most public hangouts) you'll be familiar with the sign, 'PLEASE DON'T URINATE HERE. BY ORDER'. And it just so happens that when you see this sign you suddenly feel like taking a leak. Not to worry. The sign means the exact opposite. Draw closer and you'll notice that area has been properly fertilised with urine from months and years ago. So, what do you do? Take a leak, of course! That's what the sign says, remember?

As you travel in your car you pass a sign with the graphic indicating NO U-TURN. And then the nearest U-turn isn't for another five kilometres. What do you do? Slow down as you get to the sign and navigate the bend off your lane into the next lane to continue your journey.

Keep driving and you'll see the speed limit sign. This does not mean slow down to below 65/hour. Nada! Drop your foot on the throttle and ensure you break the land speed record before your demise.

There are numerous signs littered all over that point you what to:

BUY YOUR KEROSENE HERE: It's not yours, so buy it!

PLEASE, KEEP ABUJA CLEAN: Drop refuse here

ONE WAY: Two way

KEEP RIGHT: Stay left

SLOW DOWN. MEN AT WORK: Speed on. Slow men at work

15km/hr. ZEBRA CROSSING AHEAD: Ignore it. It is in the zoo

L-plate on a car: a professional driver without a licence

'Long Vehicle': over take and get nudged off the road!

FAST LANE: Keep to 25 kilometres per hour

SLOW LANE: Minimum speed 200 kilometres per hour

When a traffic officer says stop, put your foot down; when he says go, drop it on the brakes. This is because this rule applies to drivers at the flank junctions. Reversed, your go means their go and likewise for the stop signal

There are other signs however which can be ignored at one's peril:

MILITARY ZONE. NO PARKING: Trespassers will be shot

NO SMOKING: Do it where you won't be seen

SWITCH OFF ENGINE: Applies only to second-hand vehicles

11. What is your faith?

A man without a religion is a man without an identity. Your faith is your life. It determines how you beat your wife, when to go clubbing, how to gamble, what to eat, how to say 'no' to idolatry and 'yes' to adultery, and how to chant 'peace' with a machete in your hands ready to swing. Anybody who parades himself as not having a faith in Nigeria is an idol-worshipping rascal, a Cain in the wilderness.

Nigerian has over two hundred languages and an equal number in ethnic groups. Once upon a time these warring factions would have each had their religions. But after the African Renaissance all ethnic groups were compelled to share three religions. Its followers are the Free Radicals, the Liberal Socialites and the lesser-known Centre faithful.

The Free Radical

The Free Radical is a descendant of the Great Pharisee – the race that was famed for enjoying tongue-lashings from Jesus Christ. The Free Radical belongs to an umbrella organisation, Movement for Peace, which is a front for violence. However, if you acquaint the Free Radical on this notion he'll deny the allegation.

'No, no,' he begins, counting his prayer-beads, 'the Free Radical is a man of peace.'

'But what about the killings of last month? The Police identified the perpetuators as Free Radicals'.

Pause.

'Ach! Those ones are not true Free Radicals!'

Leave the cleric in peace….

And that's the problem. The Free Radical has been misunderstood throughout centuries. He appears to say one thing and mean the complete opposite. Is it his tongue? Not likely. The Free

Radical speaks English with a tinge of Persian coated with Upper Class RP. If it's communication, the Free Radical has it at the tip of his fingers.

FR followers are democratic backwards. Women are given free will, provided they don't set foot outside the confines of their domicile; modern luxuries are barred, with the exception of mobile phones, jet-black sedans, etc.; and equity is the mantra when an opulent mansion is allowed to exist side by side with a shanty neighbourhood.

Liberal Socialites

Following closely behind the Free Radicals is the independent faith of the Liberal Socialites. The Lib Sock is notorious for his liberal ways, which is why the Free Radical accuses him of been a descendant of the lost city of Sodomy and Gonorrhoea. This has led to clashes of ideology between Lib Socks and Free Rads. Like any decent political party the Lib. Socks have a division in the centre: the Hard Right, the Far Left and the Centre.

a) The Hard Right are soft on themselves. Their place of congregation looks no less than the Taj Mahal in grandeur; any temple of less design and grandeur is considered to austere and selfish. The maxim is, 'My God is not a Poor god'. Anyone who defers from this is, is immediately branded Judas and, often, the ostracised defects to the Far Left.

Dressing for congress is delicate. Miniskirts for unmarried girls, and knee-length skirts for married women; men should appear in three-piece suits with the jacket left off. Colours should violently clash – blue trousers on brown waistcoat with chequered shirt is a favourite. This is a metaphor of expected financial prosperity, or, to use H.R parlance, 'breakthrough'.

The man at the helm of the session is a model with perfume on that a rat can pick up from the next town. He talks to the congregation in a superfluous honey-coated voice, accompanied by violent hand and leg gestures. The congregation responds to points made with a wave of the hand (with handkerchiefs attract additional blessings).

Prayer time is when to practice your *ora maximus*. Everyone should stand and show their allegiance to the faith. You may not have an ailment bothering you, and your family is fine. Get up just as well – you don't want to look a fox in sheep's wool.

Wait for the cue from the Minister before you commence prayer. And when you go raise you voice to the limit and chant a lot of gibberish. This may sound like non-sense to you, but harp on: Soul Baba has a Morse Code decoder by his side.

b) Behind the Hard Right is the Far Left. The singular acrimony that links the two is the notion that, sometime in the distant past, the Hard Right was fed up with the miserly ways of the Far Left, and moved out to form a splinter group of opposite methods. The Hard Right changed everything from God to the Book.

Meanwhile, the Far Left continued to go left. Everything that goes on in the Hard Right is the opposite for the Far Left. Dressing is conservative, prayer is in whispers and thanksgiving is a parade in strict formation. Congress is over in forty-five minutes, which is a good time to retire home for some tea.

The Centre

The Centre are where they are, which is why when someone says he's in the centre heads crank in curiosity. Because Nigerians believe in extremes (you're either Far Left of Hard Right) associating yourself with the Centre takes a bit of courage. The Centre faithful do not congregate on a particular day to share and donate to the coffers of the Minister. They are discrete, dress in regular outfits and greet each other with the tersest of nods; none of that ‘brotha’ or ‘sistah’ salutation of the *others*. Theirs is a faith of the chosen few that challenges orthodoxy in whispers and esoteric language

How to spot a Centre faithful:

i. The Centre do not have the luxury of attending congregation on the Lord’s Day

ii. The Centre does not have a dress code. Like spies they blend in with the crowd

iii. If you happen to be discussing God at a local joint, the Centre is quick to argue that there is a difference between congregating and doing good, the latter which, he posits, is more important

iv. The Centre are always brimming with energy. Tai Solarin and Ben Murray-Bruce are classical examples, to mention a few.

v. Unlike their counterparts the Centre never go by that appellation. The password is ‘traditionalist’ or ‘Free Thinker’ and most often than not you pick this out at their birthdays

In spite of the in-fighting between followers of the Liberal Socialite movement, there are curious instances where all parties have been known to unite for the common good.

When John Paul II passed on to eternal glory, Nigerian Liberal Socialites thought another election year had come and that the Supreme One should look down on Nigeria and finally give her a

Pope. Followers of the Pope, mind you, are Far Left. They began to fast and pray that the elections be rigged at the Sistine Chapel; the Hard Right, not wanting to be left out, put aside their decades-old acrimony for the Far Leftist faith and began to fast and pray for Anthony Arinze, Nigeria's only candidate in the College of Cardinals to be voted in.

During this period, I approached a Hard Right, acquainting him with the fact that the fasting and prayer going on was strictly a Far Left affair.

'Ach,' he interjected, 'is Anthony Cardinal Arinze not a Nigerian?'

No further questions, m'lord...

==

=======

When in Nigeria, humble yourself before the Master of the Congregation, and beg, 'Master, teach me how to pray'. Open your ears very well and heed:

Our Father, who art in Heaven.

Praise be to your name.

May your Kingdom come, but not like a thief in the night, lest we be caught unawares

May the mansions you have stored up for us in Heaven be done on Earth.

Give us this day our daily bread.

And forgive us our wrongs as we pretend to forgive others their wrongs.

Lead us unto temptation, only with brothers of our faith.

And deliver us from the malice of the jealous neighbour.

B. Pasturing

When in Nigeria, take time to attend the Annual Healing Session Carnival. There isn't a fixed calendar for this event, so you'll just have to keep your eyes peeled to the television for an announcement.

The commercials themselves are as dramatic as the main event. In it you see people shudder and fall as the Ministering pastor touches them with his magic finger; you see the blind hear, and the lame talk. And then the whole package is wrapped by the victorious Minister declaring to you that your year of blessing has come (don't try to understand the logic even if you get the announcement in November).

The first thing you notice when you get to the A.H.S.C ground is that it looks like a jamboree without the Boys Scout uniform. Somewhere at a high pedestal you notice a pop star in prim white suit, silver tie and immaculate shoes. He nurses a microphone.

'Excuse me,' you enquire from a brotha, 'where's Pastor Christian, the Ministering pastor?'

'Das him there'.

I see, you realise, educated. The pop star *is* the Ministering pastor. Anyways, no time gallivanting about. Settle down to the carnival....

You may be used to healing sessions in your country if you're conservative. These usually occur behind closed doors and by a secret cult of exorcists that is centuries old, speaking Latin to Persian demons. Or, for the *other* side pastors politely appealing to the demon to leave their host ('Hey, demon,' goes the fellow, 'leave that man'. And the demons pack up their suitcases and catch the next bus out).

In Nigeria, the healing session is an all-form martial arts tournament involving metaphysics and invisible projectiles. After two days of preaching, Pastor Christian (or Chris for short) calls for volunteers. He does this by declaring that certain people gathered at the carnival have demons bothering them and that such demons can only be exorcised by their hosts coming forward to the podium. Even before Pastor Chris has finished speaking a battalion of demon-hosts begins to advance. A few metres away from the podium and the miracle of miracles happens: Pastor Chris swings his arm in manner of throwing an invisible projectile. The actors… sorry, hosts, in unison respond with a Mexican wave – only this time to the ground. They pant and shudder as the demons struggle to pack their things and leave. Meanwhile Pastor Chris is making for them, reeling out a rendition of words and phrases that seem appropriate for scrambled messages from an old telegraph. The more he blabs the more you shudder, until, after an hour or thereabout, he declares the session over with a repetition of the words, 'Thank you, father'…

At this point you must resist the temptation to applaud and whistle in appreciation. This is not a show. It is a well-choreographed ceremony. Peace be with you.

Soul Baba

In the beginning, God made man. In the end, Man will make God. Between these eras, however, Man will indulge.

Soul Baba is the Nigerian equivalent of the Divine Deity. He shares some titles with the conventional Deity, but make no mistakes, he's original and worshipping him is no different from trying to understand the nature versus nurture debate.

Fast Forward to modern times. Nigeria is on record as having the fastest number of churches to spring up. Has anybody wondered why? Not at all. As long as there are enough worship houses to go round things might as well be okay. If you're coming into the country for the fist time – and wish to patronise our worship centres – things may be a little difficult for you. Which church do you attend to practice your dogmas? The most important thing to note is that if you're a stiff Conservative in Nigeria, forget it. Your conversion to the other side is imminent. Soul Baba will not have the white man's way of doing things!

When you pray request—no, order—Soul Baba around. That's what he's there for. Soul Baba has an elite commando unit waiting for orders every second. In your prayer, don't say, 'Thank you , Lord, for you are so good…'. That is noise to the Big Chief. Rather, put forwards your enemies (whoever they are) and order thus, 'Holy Ghost Fire them!' If you say this sort of prayer often Soul Baba is sure to bless you with prosperity. Mind you, this doesn't mean peace at home or joy in your work. Among other things, prosperity connotes a chain of cars, intimidating houses spread across the country, orderlies at your beck and call, and so on. When your co-religionists ask the secret of your wealth admit, 'We thenk God'.

Just to ensure your *neaveau-riche* status stays where you want it to be, be sure to constantly offer the prayer, 'Poverty is not my potion'. Soul Baba will then direct *that* potion to another hapless person who doesn't fortify himself…which may explain the numerous vagrants tramping about.

Worshipping Soul Baba

First, the revelation. This is very important. Any serious pastor without the Revelation is not worthy to serve Soul Baba. The Revelation is not what Saint John of the Apocalypse saw. This one is different. Literally, the Revelation is the effect of a cause, which in most cases is hunger. The Revelation may occur any time of the day, but be sure that it is in the morning after having a horrendous nightmare that you decide you have seen the light. After this attestation of faith, it is time to get to work.

Each time you meet your friends be sure to attract puzzlement by announcing to them that the fellow they knew as their comrade is gradually slipping away, giving way to a new you. Meanwhile, in the backdrop acquaint the owner of a two-storey flat and offer him a deal of using his abandoned garage. If you use the right approach (accompanied with the sad, lachrymal eyes of a submissive dog) you have procured a 'church'.

Start by holding service at strategic hours – when others are returning from Mass or Service. Employ one or two girls who are heavily endowed at the rear and forward regions. This isn't temptation; it's a smart advertorial targeted at potential male followers….

In time, your little garage will begin to enjoy patronage, largely because the boys want to see *your* girls. After awhile begin to solicit offering from your followers ('it is the Lord who says so', will be your reason). Aside from the loot which will go into your pocket, squeeze out some to have a local signboard erected….

Fast forward into the future and you have procured the services of bodyguards to keep agents of the devil – literally, jealous members of your worship centre – at bay. Mind you, christening your worship centre should reflect your motives: Soul Baba detests humility. House of the Rock, Inc. is a fine choice…or even Peculiar Peoples Centre, Ltd.

Every Sunday be sure to remind your hypnotised followers that the night before you had seen a vision from Soul Baba who notified you that *somebody* in the congregation was going to buy for him- or herself a brand new sports car. Forget about details. The night before may have been spent at Choices Tavern beer spot…the congregation will respond accordingly.

By now, you would have built the Taj Mahal. It is now time to reap where you have sown. Like a cardinal anointed Pope a change of name is essential. If you were Mister Saleh Kayode Ada Uzor-James, place a classified that you now wished to the addressed as Pastor James Miracle,

PhD. Soul Baba provides all: it is possible to have a PhD even if your last qualification was a Secondary School-leaving Certificate!

There is another variant of the Soul Baba fellowship (after all, he's schizophrenic). Soul Baba's Hyde character is a lonely deity who is ever ready for his followers to conquer in his name. This doesn't mean he can't do things for himself…he just loves a good fight. Therefore, fight! When you hear an infidel as much as impugn the name of one of his priests be sure to pick the machete and go on a wild spree, during which you burn everything, loot the shops and chant slogans perceptible only to Soul Baba. Then, after the carnage it's time to be politically correct. Declare to the beneficiaries of your cleansing that you meant no harm: your religion is one of peace…*A'ameen!*

12. Home Movies

It has been said that the Nigerian film/movie industry is ranked third largest in the world. However, it seems that film buffs don't know the reason for this (or the criteria which the ranking was fixed), and even those who know just mention it as though they were referring to a gnat!

Ask a film critic pacing his way down Fleet Street which film industry is rated third largest in the cinema world and he'd most likely answer, 'Third largest? Wouldn't that be…er, what's called? Lollipop?'

'Nollywood', you correct him.

'Ah, yes. That'. And he's off as quickly as a lad scampers from a stranger. If you're a Nigerian journalist out to press him to spew some more details on the issue forget it. He's done talking from the time Queen Victoria skipped her oats!

Strange.

Nigerian movies litter every movie vendor across the Continent and all we get is a few brief words of appreciation? No fair! If China is known for gung fu fights over poor American voice dub-overs, then Nolly (something), having come thus far, should have reached icon status, yes?

As a patriot, I have taken it upon myself (and anyone who cares to be Simon of Cyrene) to elucidate the phenomenon that is the Nigerian film industry.

Great things start from small beginnings. But in Nigeria small things start from great beginnings. It's about 18.54, local. The 7 O'clock news is in six minutes and you're already couched after having a bath of cold water to wash off the sweltering heat. The television set in front of you is showing indigenous music. Your children are also in the lounge, while your ever hard-working wife shuttles between kitchen and living room. Suddenly a bolt blasts through the television screen. Ordinarily, you would bolt. But you don't. You relax. It's an ad for the latest Nollywood blockbuster, with the usual retinue of stars who have featured in over five-hundred home videos shot and released in the last two weeks. By the time the ad is through you'd have sat through the entire film in just two minutes. It is now up to your housewife to send her ten-year old ingrate down to the local rental the following morning to fetch the 18-rated movie.

Titles of Hollywood movies can be misleading. You hear films like *All is Quiet on the Western Front*, which is actually about a lot of noise in the backyard; *Omen* about Amens; *A Bridge too Far* which chronicles the battle on a bridge not too far from the Studios…and so on. This titling has made Nigerians, who are very disciplined simpletons, to get the whole plots about Hollywood blockbusters all wrong. When *The Matrix* was released on media a lot of Nigerian students thought it was a CD-ROM tutorial in Further Mathematics! This debacle has led our thoughtful home video mafia kings…sorry, producers, come up with a solution: titling films as the plots go. How apt. Aside from the case, the one way to tell a Nigerian home video apart from the other lot is to pay no attention to the titles:

Sisters' Act: About sisters acting out

The Last Idiot: About the first wise man

Silent Night: Noisy afternoons

Secret Society: About an open club

Latest Boy in Town: featuring a snazzy chap in 60s outfits oppressing every girl in the village

Coming to Africa: Going to America

Most Wanted: *Set it Off* on steroids

How to Make a Nollywood blockbuster

Lights, Camera…and Go!

The making of a Nollywood movie is not as intricate as hiring a team of CGI artists or commissioning Vangelis to come up with a score. Like the name implies it is a home video. The main difference been who appears on the screen.

Step 1. Assemble your cast. This is as easy as is gets

Anybody who feels like it can assemble cast and crew (amateurs, mind you) and churn out six movies in a week (that's five working days. The weekend is designated for general release).

To attract tape sales however, be sure to get performers who have been at it for decades. You're sure to win the hearts of their fans. From hero to villain to gatemen must be a famous face. Let nothing to chance…or to a potential for that matter!

Step 2: Pick our location. This is the easiest bit. Your story has a linear plot, so be sure to follow the word literally. Shooting will be the shortest distance between two points: a village and a city. The latter *must* be Lagos, otherwise your story will make little sense to we simpletons

Step 3: produce the movie. Working with a clique of marketers is your sure way to fame. They say who gets what, when and how. Follow orders like a lackey that your are. If they ask you to throw out a professional and inject an amateur into a role don't argue.

CENSORSHIP. When making your film remember the censors. Be sure that even if your script is family-friendly the censors will stamp a big bold red '18' on it. Therefore, your home video should be laden with plot devices like witchcraft, voodoo ceremonies, visits to the haunt by night, and so on. By the time the censors get your screening copy all they have to do is *not* review it before stamping the numbers '18' on it.

TITLING. Aha, here comes the best bit. In the course of writing your script – which is about a wife-beating husband – you decided to come up with something arty. 'The Dark Side of Man' was your working title, and you looked at it and saw it was good. But your marketers screeched into the picture (pun unintended) and shook their heads violently. On release day your video has been christened 'The Bad Husband' for easy digestion by the throng of simpleton fans. Sob

PHOTOGRAPHY. When shooting, remember you are not making 'Jaws' or 'Pulp Fiction'. Nigerians are notorious for drooling over simple things, so keep your photography simple. When shooting an action scene be sure to have your characters run about in slow-motion even when the action is ten minutes away. When the shoot-out does start make sure you capture on-lookers in the background. This tells the viewer that the action is live.

COSTUMES. The average home video is actually Fashion TV on portable media. In one scene along with dialogue running into five minutes your characters have to alternate costumes, especially when it is obvious they have not moved from a spot.

SHOOTING. Why shoot on film when video will do just fine. It may deny you of entry into the global cinema and those international film festivals which could boost your film repertoire, but who cares anyway? There are tens of hundreds of video pirates waiting for your copy to hit the market.

And when you shoot, remember that Nigerians have a reputation for short-cuts. The maximum time allotted for shooting is five working days. Shorter records exist and constantly win the applause of the marketers.

DIALOGUE. Allow your characters blab on about a topic until the viewer is run down without even realising it. It's video, remember? You can always head to the nearest store and get an analogue cassette for N100 or digital tape for N500.

13. Fix me this, fix me that

Curse the day the first automotive was invented. That's what comes out of the Nigerian's mouth while he sits under the hot sun at the mechanic's shed. Maintenance is a regular feature of any mechanism, like what a medical check-up does to the human body. By default it should then be a pleasant thing. Ha! Not in Nigeria it isn't! Any self-respecting Nigerian worth his salt knows that when it's mechanic time it's hell time. Here's the reason why:

You drive a 1972 Lamborghini Miura, bequeathed you by your father who enjoyed the fast life. It's a classy sports car that leaves the residue of your super-ego in its wake, leaving stiff girls swooning inside themselves, and the boys reeling with envy.

Then, at the odd hour, the beast decides it has had enough. It breaks down at – of all places – a roundabout. Curses! You turn at the ignition, revving at the same time but the car says no go. Meanwhile, you're holding up traffic and the horns from other drivers are enough to signal a battalion out for reveille. You respect yourself and get down to push the car out of the roundabout. Hours later, you're at the mechanic's – having successfully camouflaged your snazzy vehicle as a beat-up Volkswagen Impala, to avoid questions from your throng of female admirers.

Dateline: Mechanic's shed. The sun is on the beat. The mechanic, who is easily recognised as a shady-looking fellow with unkempt hair and grease and motor oil soil dotted all over him, has opened the bonnet of your power horse and began to touch this and that. Notice the way he identifies the problem:

Step one: opening of the bonnet and touching this and that

Step two: Getting behind the wheels and firing up the car (somehow it starts)

Step three: Revving to ear-piercing level

Step four: returning to the engine to touch this and that

After awhile, your impatience takes the better of you. You approach, having hidden yourself someplace inconspicuous. You enquire from the fellow what the problem is. His tools speak first, then thus him:

'Oga, you go change the kick-starter…'. Actually, you did suspect that from the first f*** up, but you decided to let the expert handle it, which is a foolish thing really in this country. Meanwhile having told you the fault he has returned to touching this and that, his tools sending some sort of Morse Code to and fro the engine. Patiently you ask how much a new one will cost. Now here is where things get complicated. It should be a straight thing of it cost such and such and can be had in the next quarter of an hour. But this is Nigeria, and in front of you is a Nigerian mechanic. He leaves his knocking about and leans on the edge of the bonnet (Notice: this harmless action will later leave an indelible motor oil palm-print on the sands of time…), 'We fit get the Taiwan own and the Belgian'—Ah, now here's where things go Aladdin. Belgium and Taiwan? Your car is Italian, and you put this to the illiterate technician. 'Which wan come be dat?' he retorts harmlessly, before continuing, 'di wan wey dey dis wan (he motions at your car in feigned condemnation) no go last. So we suppose to put new wan'.

The news hits you as cleaver chops beef. It would be perfectly reasonable to have the kick-starter replaced with a new type. But the mechanic has mentioned Belgium and Taiwan, eliminating the Italian option. And when a Nigerian mechanic doesn't mention an option that you have in mind, forget it. That country is not worth its grease in the automotive spare parts business.

'How much be the Belgium own?' Thus you, having conceded.

Delay. Deep thinking.

'Bring one-five make I go bring am come'. Thus him.

'What about the Taiwan?' Again you.

Delay. Deep thinking.

'Dat wan na two-thousand'.

You then put it to him that the difference is only five hundred Naira, and that it implies that the Taiwan-made kick-starter is the better of the two—he cuts you off. 'Ahh, masta. No be so-o!' You retract; he explains: 'Taiwan na fake-fake dem dey sell. E no dey last,' he chastises, 'na Belgium you suppose to put for your moto. Dat wan na original dem dey make'. Each man is the expert of his profession, you concede, before squeezing out cash that you were planning on spending elsewhere. He collects the money. But he doesn't proceed to get to the nearest spare-parts vendor. He bypasses you and you follow to see him going to attend to one of the numerous broken-down cars in his shed. You follow at a pace, trying to tell him you don't have all day.

'Oga, relax,' he consoles you as he gets to a beat-up saloon with one side raised by a relic jack, with two tyres missing. It is either you're too fatigued to put up any further suggestions or voodoo has worked. Either way you find you are uncomfortably seated under the shed, making you a *bona fide* member of the Association of Vehicle Owners Under the Shed. This is an interesting union where tales of woe are swapped and consolation sought and found for hours on end.

After about what seems a century the mechanic returns with a brand-new kick starter from Belgium. In its pristine condition it looks like an unexploded ordnance from WWI, soiled with grease and paralysed by rust. He presents it to you for inspection. On your part you have to act like a mechanic's son. Ask why it has rust on it, why this is missing and what is it about the Belgians and inefficiency? Didn't they learn from *ze* Germans?

The fellow doesn't install the kick starter right away. He circumvents your car and begins to attend to another, which all the while was cleverly camouflaged to fool you into thinking that you were first in line.

Eventually the Belgian kick starter is installed. You take the honour of starting the monster, but alas it doesn't respond. You turn at the ignition and throttle like a tramp but the answer is a few coughs that ignite and then dash hopes. Wes the matter, you enquire from the oil-stained artisan. But he doesn't answer, partly because he has perched himself over your bonnet. You go to meet him and discover he is in a state of mourning. You lower your head as well in respect for the dead. After the ritual, he raises his head to reveal, 'Oga, your fuel pump is bad. Das why e no dey catch'....

When a repairman attends to your defective machinery or appliance be sure that when he does return it from that moment onwards will be a litany of problems. The repairman himself has a register-book so that when you show your face at his shack he greets you with the familiar, 'Ah, customer. Well done, sah'. Innocuous as it may sound it is actually a code-word for ticking against your name in his book.

'I have a problem', thus you.

'Okay', he says, attending to a defective piece of equipment.

You put it to him – as Nigerian lawyers do – that the last time he fixed the capacitor of your device upon reaching home the fuse burnt out. If you have announced your complaint properly he'll mumble something to himself. After what appears to be a ritual he drops what he has and takes what you have. Next comes the anaesthetic. He then unscrews and opens up the device. He attaches electrodes to the fellow to take a pulse. You wait. No pulse. Is it dead? The doctor shakes his head. He tried, but your device couldn't make it.

'Oga,' he says, taking off his surgical mask and gloves, 'this thing is dead', and he points at a tiny bit of circuitry whose damage is the singular cause of your device's untimely demise.

'How much for a new one?' you enquire. Before responding he re-screws and presents the late device to you.

'Oga, just buy a new device. Because the price of a new circuit is short of a new device by just 200 Naira'. Reluctantly, you take his advice. You also bequeath to him the dead device for him to extract the parts as scrap.

Weeks later you're buoyant enough to obtain a brand new device. As you pass by his shack you notice that your dead-and-gone device is alive and well and performing functions for him. Alarmed, you quiz him for an explanation to this puzzle.

‘Ah, oga,’ he begins, ‘ I repair am’.

Feel free to entertain a question mark over a head in the accompaniment of pity.

14. Protesters Union of Nigeria (PUN intended)

Beware the Protesters Union of Nigeria, or PUN. Many have gone, few are chosen. Foreigners who have dared impugned the Federal Republic or any thing its stands for have had to contend wit PUN. Protest-marches become the order of the day. Strikes are declared. Workers down tools and up weapons. Slogans are chanted. And in the end the Federal Government issues a query to the offending party. But, what happens afterwards?

In hard-left countries like Venezuela a comment in the right direction by any as much as an associate of the West is sure to attract the stiffest penalty. Diplomats are the luckiest: they get spirited away in the dead of night while a crack unit of commandos approaches the embassy vicinity. The lesser mortals are treated to the comfort of interrogation and, eventually, some explanation as to the whereabouts of the person now declared missing. Zanu-PF has a more ceremonious way of doing it: they give you a hell of a thrashing and then allow images of your swollen face to be beamed via satellite and on Youtube to the rest of the world…and you may not necessarily have a name that begins with Morgan.

Nigeria is not a hard-left country; neither is to the Centre or to the Right. Which explains the actions of PUN at times. PUN responds to anything that hurts the pride of Nigerians. When Jeffrey Archer Koinange, the notorious ex-CNN reporter with a cool Planet-of-the-Apes hairdo, reported in the early days of the New Republic that Nigerians were fed up with the pace of democracy *viz* development and that the Army should move in again, Koinange had asked for it. PUN swung into action. Every street corner, every beer joint, every idle office hour became the battle ground. Protest-marches were not made, slogans were not chanted and nobody bothered with the traditional placard. But, PUN was acting. Koinange's head was called for, and grumblings suggested the CNN Lagos office be shut down and the Americans driven away for making such a sweeping statement about Nigerians, who loved democracy. Cable News Network knew what to do. Within hours, the Judas was spirited out of Nigeria – CIA-style – and asked to cool his heels in Kenya. The Nigerian government itself heaved a sigh of relief, for a major crises had been averted.

Weeks after Koinange's movement, Nigerians at street corners, beer joints and idle office hours began to murmur, 'With the way the government is doing things, corruption, sodomy and tribal sentiments…I think the Army should come in to restore balance….'

'?'

Jeffrey Koinange's misadventures were far from over. Secret documents show that while in Kenya, the wily reporter began to pitch ethnic group against ethnic group (this would later lead to the infamous election crises of 2008). The CNN had had enough of this crony; unceremoniously, Koinange was dismissed. Members of PUN, long time fans of CNN, gradually began to notice the reporters conspicuous absence in reports concerning Africa.

Foul! they cried. PUN swung into action. The slogan now became, 'Racism: CNN sacks black brother!'

How time flies….

Becoming a member of PUN requires does not sense of humour; just a tinge of irony will do. Hail Caesar today, plot his downfall tomorrow. You may call it the Judas Paradox.

'The Revolution' has become a popular catchphrase in the country. It is the excuse of hope the Nigerian clings to when the going gets rough and the rough stop going. At every PUN joint, members of the radical group comment on the failings of government and map out strategies on how to effect change by violent means. These meetings run for hours even days, with an accompaniment of cold beer. To understand how the Judas Paradox works acquaint a member of PUN with arms and munitions, etc, telling him the hour is at hand. He'll chant, 'Freedom at last. Power to the people!' and all what not. By the time you've prepped yourself, Commando-style, and advanced you notice you are alone in the advance. You turn around and there's the PUN member…fifty metres away.

'Wes the matter? Les move!' you urge

'Lead on, friend,' he mutters, 'I'll follow behind you'.

=======================================

Talk the Talk

There is a splinter group of PUN, and one which every Nigeria is initiated into from birth without the consent of the consenting parents. Like any fraternity this group has a name, stylised into an acronym: CAN – Commentator's Association of Nigeria, the motto been 'I CAN'.

Following the motto, loosely cemented on Barack Obama's election catchphrase, members of this fraternity have demonstrated time without count that 'we cannot!' Like PUN the weapon of talk is choice…er, the weapon of choice is talk.

If the Federal Government wakes up one morning, brushes its teeth and announces to the unsuspecting masses that there's going to be hike in pump price of petrol, CAN will go to work. Public servants, petty traders, idle students and mechanics will begin a series of acrimonious and sour comments directed at the government. CAN will talk until someone somewhere suggests, 'Let's stage a protest to challenge the Government's decision'. At this point a good member of CAN then counter-suggests, 'Protest? Against the Government? (shrug of the shoulder) How will that work?'

And before the rebel attempts to put forward his argument he is shushed with another elderly advice: 'Don't worry. Let's just buy (petrol) at the new price…what can we do? At least God is there. He will hear our cry'. And with that citizens will delightfully queue up in long snakes to buy petrol. But even in the queues the talking has not ceased…in muffled tones, however: nobody wants a saloon with blacked-out windows parking in front of his house by night!

The top shots are not exempt from membership of CAN. When a case of (adulterated) paraffin explosion at a locale is reported on the news the Governor constitutes a seven-man committee to investigate the immediate and remote causes of the tragedy, mandated to report within two weeks. After four weeks a 60-volume report in blue laminated covers is submitted to the Governor. The Chairman of the Committee and His Excellency shake hands, smile into the cameras and sit to give a press briefing.

The following month another paraffin explosion is reported. The Governor comes on air, talks and then resolves to get to the root of the matter, to leave no stone unturned. How does he executes this? He sets up an eight-man committee....

These members of CAN are called the Jacks of all Tirades. Whenever there's a problem requiring a solution they gather in a conference room, bang heads on the issue, queue up at a buffet, crack jokes over wine, and disperse. The following week, the same thing happens again... a conference-seminar-workshop is called.

15. Committee of the Whole

I was traveling by bus to Jos. As is usual I detest long hauls and the one remedy is for me to sleep the journey through, and wake up with just a few kilometres into the last stop. But this fateful day was to be different. It was my rite of passage, the day I would be introduced to the Nigerian Jack-of-all-Tirades.

'Jesus Christ!' a woman behind me exclaimed. This is not unusual in a Nigerian bus. It is very natural for women who belong to the Hard Right faith to chant expletives during a journey. The trick is to pay more attention to the tone of the interjection; and paying attention to the buxom madam I knew it was no ordinary day. I opened my eyes from my slumber and true enough, ahead of us, was an accident scene. Slowing down we all saw the mangled chassis of a bus that had veered off the road in a barrel spin. In the true Nigerian spirit of brotherliness the driver of our bus brought the vehicle to a stop. Like a stampede we all got out, pushing and shoving. I tried to take my time out – more because I was eager to get to a clearing to ease myself – but the big madam behind me would not have my gentleman's way.

'Hurry up, my friend,' she urged, squeezing herself between seats to get her enormous weight out of the bus, 'can't you see we want to get out?' (She saying 'we' was correct – she weighed at least three wrestlers)

Eventually, she got out before me, and by now a semi-circle had been formed around the mangled bus. Now, I'm not particularly blessed with height, and trying to look over people's shoulders seemed quite a Herculean task. Defeated, I proceeded to head for the nearest clearing to take a leak, hoping that by the time I got back the ensemble would have disassembled, allowing me my own space to *spectate*. Seconds later I was at the scene, and the sympathisers had loosened a bit.

'Ooh noo,' the madam was crying, 'it is the hand of the Devil'. I took it she was referring to the accident. I arced my head to see if I too could spot the hand of the devil on the bus. But there was none.

'It was careless of the driver,' began a fellow in Salvation Army regalia.

‘How do you mean?’ I managed to enquire.

‘Overloading! Simple!’ came the answer.

But from another section of the sympathisers came a challenge: ‘It seems to me it is the axle weight. And that as the driver was trying to avoid an oncoming vehicle he swerved and entered the bush’. It is important for me to note that the we had been driving on a dual-carriage way, and I’m busy asking myself how on Earth another vehicle would have been ‘oncoming’ on *this* side of the motorway…

‘I agree,’ thus another expert, and he motioned invisible skid marks on the road, ‘the bus barrel-spun eight times. It means it was on high speed’—

‘Obviously’, I remarked. But the buffoon didn’t even get the sarcasm and instead re-remarked, ‘das right!’ in appreciation of my ‘solidarity’. Meanwhile the buxom madam was beating her breasts and uttering esoteric expletives which sounded like various names of the god she worshipped. The driver, who had finished his inspection parade of the bus returned to us, shaking his head.

‘This is bad. Truly bad. The Road Drivers’ Union keeps warning these drivers to keep to the speed limit but they wouldn’t listen’—if I recall well, we had barely left Minna than this same driver hit the 120 kilometre *per* hour mark!

‘Yes,’ agreed another Pharisee, ‘this over-speeding is not good. Even myself when I drive I make sure not to exceed 120 km/hour’. The speed limit is 100 per hour.

At the end of the solidarity exercise, and with great reluctance, we all began filing back into our bus. And the commentary continued until we had left the mangled bus as a dot in the distance behind us. One fellow dialled someone I suspected was his fiancée: ‘Darling, it was terrible,’ he was narrating into the cell phone, ‘terrible, terrible accident like that (pause). Yes. Along Minna—Jos route. Red bus. Everybody died. Nobody survived…’ (wonders in this country, I mused. So there are actually accidents where *every*body dies and there are a few survivors!). The fellow was still narrating his ordeal at the scene, sharing thanks to God that it wasn’t *his* bus that was not involved, *et cetera.* And the journey continued without a hitch. Nobody bothered to call the Road Safety authorities and even the driver who had inspected the mangled bus didn't properly ascertain how many were dead, who could be helped put of the wreckage, etc. But of course, the fellow writing down this piece is not absolved from the iniquities of the Jacks-of-all-Tirade; the spectator and the footballer make the match.

16. All for One, One for None

The Party is supreme. No doubt about that. The Party determines who gets what, when and how.

Years after the Cold War, Nigerian politicians still practice what made that era infamous: defection. And, this happens at every junction. In the UK where party fellowship is based on the founding ideology of the group, defection would be a serious crime. In Nigeria, defection is a sport. This is because party ideology is a thin layer of Vaseline insulated with PVC.

If the Americans wish to ruffle the Her Majesty's government all they have to do is throw a cat among the pidgins of English politics, whereupon the Labour MPs will begin to slug it out with their Conservative opponents, while the Liberals play the role of a certain bald, demon-eyed Italian referee notorious for his red cards. And all and sundry will begin to haggle over such trivialities as education for the Middle class, more tax for the elite, tea at board meetings, and many other English past-times.

If the Americans wish to ruffle the Biggest Black Nation all they have to do is to offer a pornographic sum of money – properly wrapped in a hold-all we like to call 'Ghana Must Go' – to any politician who as much as agrees to allow USAID install a secret satellite-monitoring gadget in his ward cleverly disguised as a water hand-pump in a backwater town.

Before long the ruling party's technocrats will begin making television appearances; the Opposition (literally, anyone *opposed* to the ruling party's *own* way of embezzlement) likewise, all making a case for or against the project. What the debate means is a struggle in line of which party's ward the beneficiary back-water town will fall under.

It is common knowledge that Democrats are meek, idle-worshipping Black-American-loving politicians; and that Republicans are craggy-faced Nebuchadnezzars whose budget reads: a) WAR b) WAR c) MORE WAR….

But in Nigerian the slate is different. The motto is all for one, one for none. In other words, the 'all' is the pot of loot at the centre, also known as 'the National cake'; and when the winner of an election takes it, he takes it all, hence the last part of the motto.

Observe the manifesto of the following parties to get the dog-eat-dog notion that politics is about:

Pee Dee Pee: Water, Stable Electricity, Food, Free Education

A.N Pee Pee: Stable Electricity, Food, Free Education, Water

Dee Pee Pee: Food, Stable Electricity, Water, Free Education

Thus, when a party manages to out-rig another at the electoral office its government is no different from what the vanquished had in its manifesto. And that's when the whistle blows. Officials in Party B, having fed on roast plantain the night before and feeling the urge for a little extra cash, decide that their party is not the answer to Nigeria's problems. The party secretary draws a laundry list of complaints against his comrades, among which is the notorious 'anti-party' activity. If this man plays his cards well, Party A – the ruling party – calls him into their fold.

B: The Theory of Ascendancy

In the 1930s the Yiddish hermit Albert Einstein shocked the world with three letters, a sign and a number: $E=mc^2$. This construction said, among other things, stated that a rocket fired.

Sometime after Independence, Nigeria contributed another formula to the world of science. It is unfortunate that the Royal Academy in the UK and MIT in the US have not recognised this achievement, 40 years into it's foundation. So, for those still ignorant of this theory, here is an apotheosis:

The Theory of Ascendancy is the only scientific statement where there are practitioners and these practitioners are a cabal. Odd? Only for an outsider. The Theory of Ascendancy is not for all; it is for the privileged few known in Nigeria as 'the elite' – literally, any body without a good education and the mettle to lust for power with a motorcade of cars to boot.

The formula for the theory is 1+2+3+4=X. To understand this formula you must understand the quest for power – politics.

Take the average party faithful. He belongs to a hierarchy which constitutes the Party Activist, the Party Faithful, the Party Stalwart, and the Party Chieftain. On a faithful day this party faithful, having eaten his girlfriend's best meal yet, approaches a Party Stalwart with a plea. He announces he is a patriot and that he has seen the light: he wants to be leader to heed the cry of the oppressed masses. This is actually a coded way of saying, 'my turn to partake in the looting is nigh, yes?'

If the faithful chooses his words wisely he may hit the bull's eye. His practice of the Theory of Ascendancy may have just begun. The Stalwart takes the proposition to the Board of Trustees, who pass it on to the Chieftains. The Chieftains whisper a few esoteric phrases to themselves. From here, the Founding Fathers – a shadowy cult – have to be in the know. Once they give their blessing to the proposition, the command goes back round the chain.

In the West it is not uncommon to see a big-shot politician retire into private life, decently falling from grace without having to chew grass. In Nigeria, doing this is the anti-thesis of your political life. Be wise. The Theory of Ascendancy is there for you to use. A local councillor becomes a local government chairman who aspires for the seat of commissioner or, if he's ambitious enough, the Governor of his state. From here the politician is armed with as many options as the muzzle of Gatling gun: if he is a well-behaved puppy of the party he could make Minister; a rebel is mad enough for the top job of President; a boot-licker (this is a radical from of the puppy) gets the compensation of Vice-president (for this position belonging to a Minority Group will be of advantage). Senators may also attempt a shot at *that* seat, although success rates have not been known to be registered. Rather, you may get to the coveted seat of Senate President, from where you may be appointed Ambassador to a long-running enemy of the Federal republic – Afric du Sud. After ten years of meritorious service, the NTA – Nigeria's very own CNN – will label you…sorry, honour you with the coveted title of 'elder statesman'. What this means is that on a whim journalists will corner you to comment on sensitive issues. A word from you could send His Excellency either cowering for pardon or despatching a unit of security services personnel to your door-step. Comment wisely.

Major League

Any serious person who wants to get the government to do justice to his domain must have the enviable quality of a Minority.

The name should not be misleading. In God's Own Second Country, the Native Indian – previously the lord of the land – is now relegated to the unenviable position of Minority. This means when he screams people close by hear him in whispers; and when he whispers people see him performing a mime. *That's* how minor the Minority have become.

In Nigeria the difference between the Minority and Majority is the difference between the King on top of the hill and the serf below. When the Minority whisper the echo reverberates across the Savannah; when the Majority cry foul, someone close by inches his head and says , 'come again…'. And that's how power goes to the people.

The ethnic groups of the Niger-Delta, agreeing to call themselves the Minority, rallied to the Government to protest the negligence of their devastated land and to demand compensation. They also resorted to armed struggled to buttress their point. The Government, not wanting to be seen to be unfair, lavished the Niger-delta people with gifts. The people tossed the gifts into the creeks and harangued, ‘encore! encore!’

Meanwhile, the North – in all meekness submitting to the title of ‘Majority’ – peacefully marched to the Government to register a complaint about desert encroachment threatening their previously arable land. The Government, with glazed eyes and stomaching a yawn at intervals, arched his head at the Majority and enquired, ‘sorry, what did you say is the problem again?’

‘!’.

If you think muscle power will do it for you perish the thought. Humble yourself into the Minority, even if your ethnic group is 2/3 of what makes up the country.

17. The National Question

Once upon a legend, there was a great giant who dwarfed all of Africa. This behemoth, Nigeria, and his enormous strength in all its goliathdom spread to all the continent. From its vocal orifice flowed torrents of black gold; the ends of the land trembled under its large feet; and people far and near generally benefited from the excrement that dropped from the giant's bowels – human resource exports.

From 1960, all seemed to go well for the giant which rode a tsunami of greatness not unlike Poseidon of old.

Then, something happened. Or was made to happen; any how, there was a happening....

The giant began to descend on its heels towards the ground. It was a slow and pitiful fall that has continued till this day. From then on, even small children who used to dread the mere mention of the name Nigerian began kicking sand into the giant's eye. All the giant could do was continue reiterating his (lost) title. This too has not stopped till today.

Today, the nation's leaders are confused. They're asking themselves, What went wrong, and *how*? To arrive at a solution, these leaders of ours have been arranging all manner of *rendez-vous*: breakfast meetings at noon, foreign seminars to solving local issues, converging in air-conditioned halls amid drinking wine and relishing multi-course meals...and so on. They call this National Interest.

After several decades, our leaders have finally found an answer to Nigeria's problems. That *answer* is a question....Hmmm.

Our bureaucrats and politicians alike have christened this project The National Question.

Don't be fooled, though. The National Question is not as simple as it looks. It is *The Da Vinci Code* written backwards! A kaleidoscope of enquiries hewn to further confusion.
The National Question is a clever way of summing the Bible, The Qu'ran and the Sutras in one paragraph! It is an excuse for big men to participate in the National Dialogue to discuss the National Problem which can be solved by the National Question to which the National Answer may be the solution.

= =

Has Nigerian always been like this?

Who fused its diverse people into the current entity?

Did Mungo Park really *discover* the Niger River even when he was welcomed by indigenes?

When did corruption become a national past-time?

Was the country once ruled by an Argentinean football maestro masquerading as a military leader?

Does all this matter?

Do we exist? Is patriotism amidst poverty relevant? Can Nigeria be spelt backwards?

Should Senators trade their 5-million naira per car luxuries for 25-million naira Humvees instead?

Is Vision 3:2020 any different from Ibrahim Diego Babangida Maradona's Vision 2000 in 1992?

Should the government secretly sabotage electrical power efforts while selling defective generators to the teeming masses?

Why are the masses teeming? Could this trend contribute to stalling the division of the national cake among the big few?

Will Nigeria survive? Are we all in a jungle with Charles Darwin presiding over tribal ceremonies?

= =

Our leaders speculate that by the time all these questions are answered, Nigerians will launched a British-made, Russian-assemble space probe from Turkey with a small Nigerian flag at the side to Mars in 2020.

18. The Sycophant

Beware the Nigerian sycophant! He's over your shoulder like an *aide de camp*. He's squatted in front of you to sing your praise. And then when you look over your shoulder he's not there. He's a voice in your head that appeals to your wallet. When you don't need him he's there; when you need him he isn't there. The Nigerian sycophant makes men; the Nigerian sycophant mars men. The Nigerian sycophant makes himself; the Nigerian sycophant never mars himself.

As a middle-rank public official you'll notice that the one thing that delays you to the office is a brigade of sycophants waiting at your gate to bid you farewell. These fellows don't possess any James Bond-style GPS device to track you. But somehow they know exactly when you leave for work (this is made all the more mysterious by the fact that the time you leave for work depends on how early or late you wake up...). On this particular day you're leaving earlier than usual, and you surmise the brigade isn't up for muster parade. Just as your gateman closes the steel doors behind you a motorcycle screeches to the front of your car. Is it a highjack? No, not all. It's the praise-singers: one rider, and two on the pillion. Before they alight, their drums are beating and their voices ringing hymns into your head. They say the things about you that are the exact opposite. They hail you as the king of the river of your village (your village doesn't even have a stream); you're the Stopper of the rain (you don't give a fig about the rain); you're the only Director among directors (first among equals in the civil service?). They rant on until you give up and reward their notoriety with a few notes. They thank you graciously, sing more songs and then let you by.

The sycophant manifests himself in another form. He's always squatted in front of your house when you're at work and when you're not at work. He's the first to welcome you from work and the last to say goodbye as you leave. At office, he may be recognised as a shabbily-dressed man in caftan, dead-pan slippers and wearing a pristine Rolex wristwatch which you as a public official can't afford in a millennia. He waits for you at the reception. As you come out, seeing off a visitor, the fellow drops to a crouch, saluting with a clenched fist and rendering a tirade of praises at you. The act is certain to take your hand to your wallet pocket, as the pest isn't prepared to leave on a whim. He takes your gift, yes, but he isn't quite through with you. As you return into your office he skulks behind you, narrowly missing the halting hand of the Personal Assistant. Once in, the old man confides in you about his family issues, how one of his daughters is getting married, how he *has* to host an Army of visitors from neighbouring villages, etc. He goes on long and hard, and soon enough he's thanking you and singing more praise as he finds his way out. Big Sigh.

Weeks later you are fingered in a financial misappropriation allegation. Observe: the very people who sang your praise ever so loyally will be the first to say, 'We knew it all along... he is one of those civil servants bringing bad name to the organisation'...

B. Applox for Him!

Every performer needs an audience. And the Nigerian is no different. Except that in the case of a Nigerian performance a special knack is needed in understanding its intricacies. For performer and audience there are conditions that must be met for all and sundry to go home blissful and happy.

The most popular (and drawn-out) performance is the speech. The speech is what it is: a speech. But to the Nigerian, the speech is an amalgam of everything. It's a valorous attempt at insulting the intelligence of those assembled before you, idle enough to be there in the first place, who have agreed that you know more than they do and are willing to make you a Caesar in small time.

If you're giving a speech in this country, you may at first be taken aback by the reaction of the audience at certain points during your delivery; the same applies for an audience outside Nigeria which is playing host to a Nigerian speech-maker. The dividing rule is the failure to observe the cardinal rules:

For both speech-maker and audience, the rules inter-twine.

As you're called to the podium by the compere, pace yourself. It would be rude to just get up and walk to the high stand. The audience will applaud at the mention of your name. This is your cue to delay and allow the clapping be your red carpet. Just as the applause is dying down get up and make your advance.

For the Audience: As soon as you notice someone get up and head for the podium, don't get tired. Applaud harder.

For the speaker: Begin your speech with an adage in the form of a joke. This is an old ritual Nigerians love to hate these days, and if you strike the right tone the audience will donate a few coughs!

After the appetiser, begin your speech. Tell your listeners that, contrary to what the compere called you earlier in the introduction, you're not the Messiah. This is snide way of professing you're the Christ! It will be taken as a good sign of humility. At this point...

Audience: Nod in appreciation without thinking. Among the ranks feel free to interject, 'This man is a guru!' 'Such a simple man'.

Speaker: Carry on. Or, as our cliché-laden journalists will say, 'set the ball rolling'. Begin by quoting a long-forgotten 'prominent scholar' whom nobody has heard of, dovetailing into its relevance in the Nigerian context.

Audience: Applaud in appreciation. You don't know who he's referring to and this is a good excuse to demonstrate ignorance.

As the speaker continues, pay attention to him and not the speech. He'll cue you when to applaud. At certain points he'll end with clichés and raise his head at you. Applaud like mad, nodding as an accompaniment.

After the speech, all rise to your feet. This is necessary even for someone who just finished school yesterday. At this point, the compere comes in. Now, the compere is as much a performer as the speaker and the audience. He is recognised as the MC, dressed in a dinner jacket in the hot afternoon and smothering the microphone like a baby. He also has a pair of non-matching shoes. At the end of the closing applause, this gentleman gets his cue to saunter forward in the wake of the speaker's departure.

'Beauriful! Beauriful!' is his own applause. And then he proceeds: 'In fact, the distinguished speaker spoke so well I don't think we did him justice (Audience, here goes again). In fact, I think the distinguished speaker needs another round of applox. Applox for him!'

Having exhausted all your palm-power, you have no choice but to obey he who is lord. Another round of applox…sorry, applause raises the roof…

Meanwhile, you as the speaker, comfortably seated, must show you own appreciation by nodding humbly. This doesn't mean anything, really. Just that people won't take kindly to your head remaining static while they beat their hands for you.

But, to return to the compere. The art of MC in Nigeria is a course not included in regular school curriculum and yet you have to attend school for it. One misfire will mar you for the rest of your life. Knowing when to slip in and slip out is the difference between a shame and fame. When I was a boy MCs were the very reason I dreaded public occasions. An event of thirty minutes could drag on for hours, even into the night. What were the MCs doing wrongly? Looking back, nothing! They did their job well. It just takes a Nigerian to understand them. The MC is the one person who plays with the space-time continuum at will, and then, at the close of that event, although your watch may read fours hours later, your body will register that only half an hour has gone by!

POSTSCRIPT. When you applaud you do not necessarily have to induce logic into it. Once upon a speech I began to drift off from the drab talk. Suddenly, there was a sudden ejaculation of hands beating. I started. The fellow seated by me seemed enthusiastic in his own show of appreciation.

'What did the speaker just say?' I asked, beating my hands as well.

The fellow shrugged and continued the ritual.

'?'

19. The Original Big man

The Original Big man is this country's by-product of the Free Market-Truism-Communist parent. The experiment, however, went horribly wrong and the result was the OBM. After the laboratory exploded the OBM infant escaped into the darkness, never to be seen again. Decades later, the OBM has grown up. But be careful. The chemical instability is still active in his DNA, so identifying him on first contact may be difficult.

The OBM's wealth is a mystery, sometimes even to himself. If you can trace Bill Gates from his humble beginnings hacking into school records and doctoring his term results, up to his first thousands, then for the OBM that is long story. Trace the source of any big man's wealth and you're sure to come up with two extremes: the Beginning and the Now.

The Beginning is the man's school days selling biscuit by the roadside and making flat-out F9s in his result sheet; the Now is when he has a private frigate sitting comfortable in his backyard swimming pool.

Pause. What happened to the time between the Beginning and the Now, you may ask. Forget it! That doesn't exist. The OBM will tell you that it does not matter how he got there but that his story illustrates how anyone (sshh. illiterate, that is) can succeed in life.

The OBM is a big man. You know him by his big car in which he carries big girls to big hotels for big romps. He lives the big life on a big post. Eventually, he dies and gets a big funeral. From there he goes to meet the Big Man and gets the big judgement.

The OBM watches an NTA News announcement appealing to the public for quarter of a million Naira for successful surgery to be conducted on a little boy who has a heart problem. He weeps, commenting bitterly to his praise-singer how the black man has become the object of pity in his own country. Touched by the little boy's plight, the following day the OBM acquaints the motor dealership in town to claim ownership of a slick Toyota Century in which he'll be chauffeured in and given time to think about the plight of the little boy….

The OBM is a man with a big heart. Making his acquaintance is vital if you're to understand the meaning of charity. Once upon a drinking session an OBM presided over ceremonies. As it was Friday, drinks were on him. Naturally everyone exploited the opportunity – Nigerians just love freebees. At the end of his session, one of the beneficiaries made to go home to his waiting wife. He confided in his benefactor to lend him fifty Naira to get transport home. The OBM wasn't too pleased with the appeal.

'What are you going home to do?' he queried.

'Oga', he began, 'It's my wife'….

The OBM waved him off. 'Look, I don't have transport money to give you. Besides why go home when the fun has just started?' And he signaled the bar man with a hiss of the mouth. 'Bar man. Please, another crate of beer for my friend here… '

A crate, mind you, costs 1,000 Naira! Notice how the OBM demonstrates his generosity: he may be uneasy when you ask for a miniscule amount of money, but is ever lavish you with a favour that costs more than twice what you asked earlier and which you will have to consume on the spot!

How to know if you're a Big man

Been a big man is not as easy as it seems. Whilst one may be to used to the Bill Gates and the Sultans of Brunei who make themselves and oppress lesser mortals into acknowledging their presence, here you're not a Big man until they say so. And who are they, you ask?

You're sitting in your car, in traffic. Along the rank a few vendors are moving from car to car, hawking their wares and tears. In a few minutes you'll know who you are...

Who you are depends on how the vendor will approach you. If you are a Big man, a vendor glides to your window, which is wound up. He knocks politely on your window as you sit in the Owners' Corner reading a daily. You manage to look up after you come to a page that has nothing to offer. The vendor smiles at you and raises a snazzy item. Again you manage to crank down to listen to what the fellow has to offer.

'Serr,' he says through his nose in a callously-rehearsed effort to mimic an American accent, ' one thousand five-hundred Naira recharge card'. The fact that this fellow is a shabbily-dressed vendor and has spoken through his nose for your sake (or for the sake of your money) then he has confirmed you are a big man. You have arrived. And since you have been recognised thus you have to act that. That'll be on hold.

Now, how to know you're a nobody: you're in the same traffic and you notice the refill-card vendor interacting with the passenger of the car ahead of you. You're hoping this fellow comes your way. I mean, everyone wants to be a big man, don't he? You beat your fingers at your steering wheel, responding to music in your head (since you don't have one of those stereo jacks). Then, from somewhere you hear the usual catch-call every Nigerian uses to summon attention: a long hiss. You hear it because your window is cranked down and you're enjoying the natural air-conditioner. Turning to your onside you see a vendor skulked up by your car, darting over his shoulder as if to make sure nobody's watching. He's holding up something that looks like a fetish, and you make concealed attempts to drive him off. He's not ready to move.

'Pst, oga,' he begins, holding up the voodoo item at your face, 'here's rat poison'....

Q.E.D

20. Adjutant, My Adjutant

It is no mystery that the Nigerian bureaucrat loves his deputy. O yes, win the heart of your boss and you're sure to inherit the Earth as surely as the meek. Every self-respecting Nigerian officer needs a deputy; every self-respecting rank and file craves a deputy. When Oga gives you an assignment, pass the job down. It's not laziness, but division of labour.

But to pass tasks down the ladder you must have a plethora of subs enough to make a human chain. For a section of the Establishment to run properly there has to be the headman: the Permanent Secretary. He is assisted by a secretary who has a Personal Assistant, who answers to the Special Adviser. The Special Adviser is in himself a small Caesar. Under him is his Confidential Secretary, who holds a leash wound around a Senior Special Assistant. The Senior Special Assistant is assisted by a Special Assistant who is in turn in charge of the Personal Assistant to the Special Assistant....

So you can see that when a job is assigned there is ladder to be descended until it gets to the very last man. And who is the last man? This remains a mystery in the Establishment. You may be fooled to assuming that the lowest of the low, the Messenger, is the last man. But by the time you enquire, 'Mallam[1], where did you keep File 4B?' he'll promptly get up, crank his head around, arms akimbo, and ask, 'Where did Abdul go...?'

[1] Arabic, 'scholar'; also sometimes used informally as an address equivalent to 'Mister'

21. The Nigerian Law & Disorder Force

No self-respecting nation can afford not to have an iconic police force that is instantly recognised by the offender and the offended; if the UK has Bobbies (who have evolved into trigger-happy Gunnies) and Los Angeles is infamous for the L.A.P.D, then Nigeria has got its equivalent in the black khaki wearing ever-friendly policeman or –woman.

Members of the Nigerian Law & Disorder Force are not known to be soft-spoken to children waiting to cross the street or to engage in gunfights and car pursuits. *An-anh!* The Nigerian Law & Disorder Force has its thing, and it is this thing that has made it stand out through the years.

At first sight, you may be tempted to identify a policeman or –woman (when will all this gender sensitivity end?) by the Lord Lugard-issue black khaki, dead-pan loafers (or its equivalent), and a beret which doubles as a makeshift money sac, with an insignia of a certain animal not usually known for its policing characteristics. But watch it, fakes abound. And you can't confidently say this person is a policeman until you make his or her acquaintance. So, here goes:

The one way to make the acquaintance of any law enforcement officer is, of course, to be an offender. In Nigeria, you have to be both offender and offended. If by any chance you're involved in a car accident and a Nigerian policeman is standing by then there's going to be a bit of a drama. Both offender and offended will be hauled to the station. The offended will be locked up and the offender will be set free. Case closed. Strange logic? That's the Nigerian police for you. Nothing really seems to add up and yet day by day they carry out their civic duties with honour and patriotism.

For any foreigner, the one acquaintance you want to make is with a Nigerian policeman. And what better place to make it than on the road. So, you're navigating your way through a typical Nigerian sub-urban road, which is no different from a high-speed F1 race. Then, at a junction you signal your intention to veer off. Unbeknownst to you, a typical Nigerian motorcyclist (a.k.a *achaba*, a.k.a *okada*, a.k.a "try and die") equally has the same intentions. But *he* doesn't signal, and the result of this impasse is an auto crash. It's a mild one and the motorcyclist is not injured. Just as you get out to exchange a few words of altercation, you notice that a policeman has lodged himself in the front passenger seat of your car. This is actually a stealth tactic taught them at the Training College. And, believe me, it would be wise not to underestimate it. So now you have a motorcyclist to argue with; but what about the policeman who is seated comfortably in your car like he's been there ages? But then, you think, this may be to your advantage after all. You circumvent the car to the other side to register your complaint.

'Officer,' you begin, 'this fellow'—

But the last thing policeman wants to do is listen to your protest. You notice he doesn't even look at your as he speaks, and when he does it's straight out of *1984*: 'We're going to the station', is all he says, and continues his stiff lounging in your car.

'What? Why?'

Your enquiry is still hanging when you notice that another policeman has engaged the motorcyclist. Where did he come from? No matter, you continue to register your curiosity with the uniformed fellow who has made you car his new post.

'My friend will you get into the car,' he barks at you, 'I say les go to station and you're shouting at me'. Shouting? When dis that happen, you quiz yourself as you register your innocence. But the constable is long through with you, and after awhile his colleague urges you to obey, that there's no problem....

Half an hour later you're at the police station. And to welcome you the woman police constable behind the counter asks you to drop your belongings. She also proceeds to write your name on a blackboard behind her, which has seen better days (just above the blackboard are encouraging assurances which should be taken for granted: POLICE IS YOUR FRIEND. BAIL IS FREE. KNOW

YOUR RIGHTS). In your puzzlement, you enquire what's going on. Watch how you ask though, for insistence attracts the answer from that famous Nigeria police side-kick known as 'talk true'. Now, the talk true is a jack of all crimes. It is cleverly disguised as a truncheon, but that's not what it is. One word from this fellow and even the hardest of criminals have been known to confess their crimes before hand! But to return to the station. Or rather, the Interview Room. The arresting constable has forged a sheet of paper and a pen, asking you to write a statement.

'Can I call my lawyer?' you request, fagged out. The PC looks dead at you. You can see in his eyes he hasn't take your comments lightly.

'Lawyer', he says with mirth, 'which wan come be dat again?' And he throws his head back in raucous, Guy Smilie-style. This is the beginning of your ordeal. In spite of your pleas all your get is a cell whom you share with the offending motorcyclist. The N.L.O.F, been so thoughtful about reconciliation, decide that a night in the cell of offender and offended is good for making up. The following morning, a friend has come to bail you out. Transports of relief. You remain behind the counter while the female constable sorts things out with the Saviour. They converse in fierce whispers and you get the feeling you're been haggled over. After awhile, your friend slips a wad of notes across the counter to the WPC.

'Hang on,' you protest, 'you said bail is free'.

'Is that so?' the WPC retorts, before adding, 'oya now, Mister Lawyer. Bail your self for free let us see'.

At this point, a lot of punctuation marks appear over your head.

As your belongings are handed over to your, you come face to face with a bill of lading. You have to pay for the pen and sheet of paper used the day before to collect your statement, the chalk the WPC used to put your name on the charge board, and feeding. The last part is essential as it is possible that the food did come into the cell by metaphysical means.

After all that it's all smiles from all and sundry staff of the station. The police loves you.

****

Warning at an American crime scene, with blood splattered here and there: CRIME SCENE. DO NOT CROSS

Warning at a Nigerian crime scene, looking innocuous: CRIME SCENE. PLEASE PASS HERE. SUSPECTS WILL BE TREATED AS PASSERS-BY; PASSERS-BY WILL BE TREATED AS SUSPECTS.

When a civilian strays into restricted territory a policeman nearby will politely signal the fellow. 'Sir,' he'll begin primly, 'this area is off limits'. And, like a good citizen, you'll apologise and be on your way.

In Nigeria, as you approach the same area, you'll hear the cock of a rifle, and the all-too familiar catch-call from a distance, 'Ssss'….At this point, don't play good citizen and wait. If you're guilty, you'll bail for it; if you're innocent you'll bail for it twice as fast. In the eyes of the Nigerian policeman you're guilty until proven innocent…and this often happens in the morgue!

The Nigerian policeman knows more than you do. Accept that and you'll be on your way to becoming their best friend. An uncle of mine was driving down in his classic Volkswagen Beetle when a policeman flagged him down at a checkpoint. The dusty-looking fellow, blood-shot, began circling the vehicle, having ignored my uncle's salutation of 'well-done'. After the law-enforcement ritual, the Sergeant stopped dead in front of the car

'My fren, open your bonnet!' Bonnet? That's the boot, my uncle suggested politely. All he got was a *sharrap!* and repetition of the order. My uncle got down and opened the boot. The Sarge gazed down into the boot, eyes popped.

'Well well well,' the Sarge began, un-slinging his rifle, 'offence lamba wan: dribing without engine!' Any protest by my uncle was futile as the officer wouldn't have it. He now directed my uncle to the back of the car to open the boot. 'But this is the bonnet,' corrected my uncle. This next pedantry was answered with the cock of the rifle (that's "come again" in law enforcement parlance). And then when the bonnet was opened, the officer repeated his neck ritual.

'Offence lamba two: driving with stolen engine!'

CASE CLOSED

CONFIDENTIAL

N.LO.F ranks are not what they appear to be. Whenever you see an OR[1] be sure to consider him an officer; ranks are always two rungs ahead. Thus a constable is actually a Corporal, a Sergeant has Superintendents as his mates, Superintendents are Inspectors-generals-in-waiting….the man at the very top is usually considered with the honours VC, MC, DSO, CBE – the Conqueror of the ****** Empire.

[1] Other Ranks – the junior cadre of most military or para-military structures, also referred to as 'rank and file', and consisting of all personnel before the rank of Lance-Corporal or its equivalent

22. Courtesy, as We Like it

Inheritance of the rules of courtesy from the British have taught the Nigerians – previously second to the Spartans – how to comport themselves, what to say, what not to say, things to have etc. I cannot confidently say what courtesy was in the time of my forbearers, largely because they didn't leave a memento; the few that have straggled into the twenty-first century have done so by word of mouth.

However, with respect to the past, I can comment on what courtesy is like in Nigeria today, and with bated breath, I shall predict that by the next century things would have changed.

The Nigerian gentleman is obsessed with the Compliance Syndrome. He himself doesn't know it yet, as even his resident psychiatrist is not ready to risk a tongue-lashing. Before we proceed, a word or two about the C-Syndrome.

Nobody knows where the C-Syndrome started, and as yet, scholars at the Royal Institute are yet to catalogue it. What is certain is that, unlike other ailments, it has a hibernation period, during which it gathers energy by the quanta. And when it does manifest it has become nearly impossible to cure. Sometimes the bearer may experience delusions that he is in top condition and that it is *you* – if you're attempting to knock him out of it – that has C-Syndrome!

C-Syndrome means you adhere to an invisible set of rules, which, according to your delusions, originated abroad. The vector continues to spread by means of the notion that the world is globalised and that compliance with these rules be adhered to lest you be left behind.

Once, I had an itch inside the caverns of my nostril and promptly attended to it. I must confess that I reacted to it rather violently. Unbeknownst to me a Nigerian Gentleman had been watching. As soon as had relieved myself this fellow acquainted me with the suggestion, 'Oga, it is not polite to pick your nose in public'.

Aside from the question mark above my head something else struck a cord: it is all right to pick your nose, then. Just don't do it where you'll be seen....

As a gentleman you must not be seen opening the door for a lady: you will scandalise yourself and embarrass the lady. Before you embark on any chivalrous venture be sure to be polite enough to wait for the help-call before responding.

It is said that eye contact is a sign of frankness; in Nigeria direct eye contact with an elder is a show of discourtesy. When conversing with a fellow who is your senior by many years be sure to keep your restless eyes elsewhere. This doesn't mean you're lying; it is giving honour to who it is due.

When dating, be sure to spend from taxi fare to taxi fare (this should be so even if you're a bicycle spare parts dealer going out with a top-class banker)

The Golden Embrace

A friend of mine who has spent many years Her Majesty's country once asked me if it was polite for men to embrace.

'Of course,' I answered, my tongue in my cheek. I was to find out later the reason behind the ridiculous enquiry: in the UK an embrace between men is impolite, and when you do see it occur a permit has been obtained from the Met Police. This has come from where the Desk Sergeant forwarded the application to the Office of the Lord Mayor who passed it on to the PM from where Her Majesty suspended her afternoon dog-walk to attend to the request. Tears rolled down my cheeks....In Nigeria we embrace every minute!

Embracing in Nigeria is the difference between being labelled a gay or lesbian. Two boys who embrace with gusto are said to be very loyal friends; an embrace by the same boys with the arms loosely wrapped about each other, however, will attract dissenting whispers.

When two girls embrace like lesbians would – haughtily, and then accompanied by various suggestive compliments of how fine her hair is, her make-up, her derrière – they are friends; when the embrace is with gusto they are suspect lesbians.

This same rule applies to the handshake. If you shake 'properly' you make yourself. As a man, make it a full Monty – clasp of the hand in a tight grip, accompanied by unabashed eye contact. As a girl, stretch your hand in a reluctant span, as though about to say hello to a lizard. And when your hand is taken allow only the fingertips to be touched. This is a good sign your are comported.

Drinks on us…

The Nigerian is not a sucker for rules about drinking. That's why he makes his own. The rules on what to drink when to drink and with what to drink is very easy to follow: just reverse everything you know about conventional drinking and you have Nigerian courtesy…on the house.

- Champagne is sipped in a tea-mug in the morning with a serviette
- Beer is gulped in a champagne flute, served with a saucer. Time: dusk till dawn
- Soft drinks can be taken with plastic cups, when receiving visitors
- Water should be absorbed not in a glass cup but straight from the sachet. Consume whenever parched

N.B. The Nigerian is a generous man at heart, compared with the French man who is horrendously courteous with his gourmet. As his comrade passes by he doesn't invite him to join in. Rather, it is upon the obsequious passer-by to say, '*bon appetite*'. The poor things!

In Nigeria you may be eating lunch paid for by your hard-earned salary… it is upon the passer-by to join you. Already you would have made provisions for an extra mouth.

However, owing to the globalisation trend some Nigerians are gradually becoming French. When you hear the invitation, 'I'm eating' don't be foolish and grab an extra piece of cutlery. You'll be met by the viperous rebuff, 'what are you doing!'

As a passer-by cum visitor therefore when you hear the clarion call hold back yourself.

'Oga join me', thus your host.

'Thank you,' thus you, 'I've just had lunch before coming'. This is actually a coded way of saying you're as famished as a road, but that you don't want to be seen to have a long throat. If you wish to know your host is sincere, he'll insists while bringing along an extra plate and piece of cutlery. At that point you may admit defeat and let fly your gastronomic incivility.

Bon appetite

23. Sex

When filling a form in Nigerian there is a portion that asks you to specify what sexual affiliation you are.

Sex in Nigeria is the ultimate taboo. Because of the level of discretion one may be tempted to assume that children are conceived via artificial insemination. Any inference or otherwise in the direction of the topic of sex attracts a fine of ostracism. If you're lucky you may get the Upper Class rebuke: 'Please… ' accompanied by a gesture of the open palm. If you're unlucky you get a verbal lynching from the neighbours who will eagerly pass your name down to the next man of your lecherous ways. Pack your things and leave the neighbourhood.

So, when you're about to fill a form that openly asks you to discuss the forbidden subject, look over your shoulder before you make the decision that may make or mar you. If, by any chance you are in a queue and your turn reaches look closely at the form at the letters M and F. Since you're in public then meaning of the letters would be the gender Male/Female.

If fortune smiles on you and you get to fill your form in the privacy of your domicile then M indicates Many (times you have sex a week); or if you're a conservative tick F (few).

Sex is responsible for secret codes flying between the sexes. When a woman lets you see into her handbag avoid her; she isn't worth the chase. Likewise a boy who is wary of who sees the innards of his wallet as he fiddles for change is said to be wise.

When a girl lets a boy embrace her on first contact it is a polite way of demonstrating fondness; she, however, scandalises herself with a handshake – an overt show of sexual interest.

DOs and DOS

Dos and Don'ts tell you what you should or shouldn't do. Simple enough. In Nigeria we have Dos and DOS (note the difference in punctuation); that is what you *can* do (in private) and what you *should* do (public):

FOR GIRLS: Never mention the subject of sex, even among your friends and when you do use Morse Code that is intelligible only to yourself.

When with your boyfriend do not confess your admiration for his beefy body among other things. You may be labelled a tart. Play cool and pretend all's well even if you're waiting to explode inside. In the thick of a *boudoir* liaison be sure to mute all responses....Upon finding a pack of prophylactics in your lover's pocket, raise hell for as much as possible. Rave on on how it is indecent to carry the forbidden item as he has done. Call him 'spoilt' to boot. However, if he wishes to make rain fall, insist he wears a raincoat.

FOR BOYS: There is a little liberty for boys. Restrict sex talk to the pub, or, if you don't drink, to odd hours of the night and with no-one else in sight.

Be sure to conceal contraceptives in areas where they are sure to meet expiration quickly: wallet, under the mattress, inside tight corners etc.

FOR ADULTS: You may have a long-overdue appointment with your GP in which case honour the call at 11 a.m, when your colleagues will be at work. As you approach the GP's office make the following security checks: surveillance cameras, hidden microphones. After you've cleared the first checkpoint proceed to knock on the door. When ushered in ensure that the walls of the office are insulated with sound-absorbing carpets and reinforced with three inches of armour.

Chat for hours on end. Ask your GP how's his wife, his children. How was the weekend, did church service go well; how about that huge refuse dump in front of his house? Did he finally get to bribe the local Sanitation Agency to come and clear the ordure?

Then, at 2 p.m, bid him happy Monday and make to leave. Then, return to your seat, lick your lips and announce in dulcet tone, 'Emm…doc, I have this problem…'. You may then unzip to show him your malfunctioned working tools.

As a parent the preaching against fornication should be top on your list, especially against your teen children. However, if you do find out that your daughter is dating a chap from a respectable home be sure to drop the act. After all, your daughter is 'dating': so much better staying in one boy's bed than jumping between several's.

For pop stars, the situation calls for political correctness. As a role-model to many jobless youths you may be asked to advice them. With the backdrop that every night after a gig is a mass orgy with your throng of female fans, advice your male followers thus:

'Be faithful'.

This does not mean be faithful to one partner. It implies *esprit de corps* to your female friends….

ADDENDUM. Sex is a thin layer. Breach it and the true picture emerges. Once upon an interview one of our home video actresses was asked to comment about candidates fraternising with movie producers to get roles.

'It is indecent,' she said, 'no girl who is worth her mettle should stoop so low just to get a role'.

The following week another newspaper reporter asked if she (the same actress) could act nude. She cranked her head, gave it a thought and replied, flat out, no!

'Not even for five million Naira?' pursued the reporter. And it was then a question mark appeared over the actress's head.

Epilogue: I Dream Nigeria…

I woke up one morning and put on the television, and on it the Heart of Africa campaign video, engineered by Tony "Heinrich Himmler" Iredia and his erstwhile boss Frankenstein Nweke Jr, was running. It is a promotional that has rivalled the national anthem, at least for upper cadre bureaucrats in the Federal Service (makes more sense to sing "Heart of Africa" than all that gibberish about "Arise, O compatriots…") and is the whistle which Nigerian leaders are using to attract foreign investors who are keen on enjoying the fastest growing tourism market south of the Sahara: kidnapping.

Is my country in a sham? Hardly. At least not at this moment of optimism. During the Second Coming of Chief Are Mu-mu Obasanjo Nigeria enjoyed so much drama that the world couldn't ignore the ranting of the young democracy. In 1999, big mobile telecoms concerns swooped on the country, selling walkie-talkies for cell phones and charging talk time fees that could pay school fees for two terms. The nation, to borrow from government optimists, was moving forward.

World Bank execs, itching to exercise a little economic espionage, advised the President to accept their token in the person of Chief Economic Spy Mistress and Strategist Ngozi Okonjo-Wahala to re-energise the Nigerian economy. Her appointment worked wonders: within months, trading at the Nigerian Stock Exchange was roping in Naira to the trillion. The trickle down effect: garri, a commonplace local staple food, bade farewell to the common man. Meanwhile, the World Bank and its cohorts drafted and published reports which gave the young democracy the thumbs up…the nation was moving forward.

However, just when things couldn't get more exciting the country was hit with its first petrol crisis since Obasanjo took over. That period, Nigerians decided to save auto energy by having petrol for breakfast and walking to work on foot. Then there was the thing with the electric corporation constantly assuming every hum in the sky to be enemy aircraft and thus shutting down power indefinitely for weeks on end (it denies the pilot targets on the ground). Apparently, the persons in charge had been in seclusion since the end of the Civil War and were still putting to practice anti-enemy aircraft drills. Until Obasanjo left office in May 2007 officers-in-charge at the electric corporation have not ceased this unique strategy.

Morning came and evening came: the Second Term. The President won a second mandate, mostly because certain opposition figures were more comfortable working as separate units rather than as a common force.

The Second Term was more laden with drama. Of important mention is the "Heart of Africa" campaign. The origin of this was that a certain western journalist disguised as a black man in the person of Jeffrey "Archer" Koinange had sabotaged motorways (among other economic and social demolition exercises on behalf of the CNN) and then proceeded to film these derelict pictures which were beamed to the world under the title "This Is Nigeria". Obasanjo, so bush-talk goes, was enraged. Summoning his assembled creation Frankenstein Nweke Jr., he promptly commissioned him to counter the foreign threat. Jeffrey didn't wait for government Land Rovers to visit his Lagos office...

Nevertheless, Frankenstein Nweke Jr's campaign was on the way. Deciding that Congo Brazzaville didn't make much use of its position as the heart of Africa he and his deputy, Tony, seized the name tag, reversed the map of Africa and proclaimed Nigeria to be the new heart of Africa. The promotional of the campaign ran with pictures of various fun spots of Abuja, cleverly packaged as "Nigeria". Hmm....

The campaign also ensured bureaucrats to speak about the country in the reverse. Thus, if a potential investor expressed fears for his life should he venture into the Niger-Delta a bureaucrat would assure him thus: 'Don't mind them. It is journalists reporting the situation out of proportion…’. An investor keen on his family would thank the fellow and board the next plane out…to Congo Brazzaville, the real heart of Africa.

I woke up again, and when I put on the television there was this man been sworn in as the successor to Obasanjo. I didn’t understand. Wasn’t it the *other* fellow who won the polls…? No matter, my revolt is within myself and I decide (because I don’t have much of a choice) to live with the new government.

Low and behold, the drama of Obass and his cronies wasn’t concluded; not that *he* was back…no. The scriptwriter of this play decided to present his performance with a different cast…think *The Last King of Scotland* with rapper Curtis “50 Cent” Jackson in the lead…!

Anyway, like a lot of Nigerians, I paid a visit to the theatre and bought myself a ticket to this performance of old wine in new skin…or is it new wine in old skin…? No matter, there’s a wine and skin somewhere…

The play began in earnest. The lead was Obasanjo’s successor, Moses Yar’ Adua with supporting roles of Goodluck “Black Hat” Jonathan, David Markus Anthony and Patricia *tete a tete* Etteh. For the first few minutes, the plot ran well. The lead character assured his throng of fans of his commitment not to have scenes of violence, sex, nudity or strong language in his mores, unlike his predecessor. The “assistant actors” did likewise, although it got a little boring when they ranted the same mantra to cliché point. Nevertheless, theatre goers generally felt the pricey ticket paid at the booth may have been worth the Naira. This spirit pervaded until the unthinkable happened: Fourth supporting character, Patricia *tete a tete* Etteh had a secret liaison with the ageing Sicilian mafia bosses and told them that she could fill their piggy banks to slot-topping level in return for a swig of the Devil’s Drink: power. The bosses named their price; Etteh played it nice. Using her hairdo to render herself invisible through a corridor of shut eyes she carted away millions of Naira, paused by two commas along the chain of zeros. The Sicilian bosses mistook Naira for Lira and didn’t bother checking before stashing it away. There was chaos afterwards. Rival gangs and the police alike haggled over the Etteh debacle. At a point, Etteh would sit atop a dais and preside over ceremonies involving gangsters shooting it out with the police. A wry smile of satisfaction would remain stretched across her face. And at the end of the salvo, she would wipe the beads of sweat that had aerosoled on her forehead and swagger a swagger out of the scene preceded by a Sergeant-at-Arms wielding a huge dildo, which Madam Speaker was to claim was integral in her massage programme.

The whole charade was becoming too much too bear for the mind, like premiering *Star Wars* to a horde of Congolese. It was at this point that I relapsed into deep sleep. I cannot now recall how or why, but it came so suddenly I didn't have the reserve energy to ascertain the remote cause ('certainly wasn't the performance; I too wanted to know how the drama would end...).

In the dream I was in a labyrinth. The background was rapturous with cheering noise, and in a moment I could see why: the '70s football skipper Socrates Obasanjo was dazzling in a warped soccer match. Many had been sceptical about his return to the turf, but in no time he had proved his mettle, as he had done back in the day. Even Ibrahim Diego Babangida Maradona could not match the skill of this aged yet active player as he was schemed out of an attempted return match into the Nigerian Football Power League. While Obasanjo continued doing his thing, in the middle of the match a white man with a long nose that could pass for a stapler rushed into the pitch (funny things, dreams) and handed the skipper a report.

'Congratulations,' the white man said through his nose, 'your country has done it again! First country south of the Sahara to get infested with bird flu. It has just been added to the Small Stout Book of World Records'. And with that the fellow proceeded to decorate Obass with a medal inscribed, "El loco senilis". Obass then proceeded to abandon his current efforts at goal and dance the dance, before been transmogrified into King Kong in *agbada*. While Obass auditioned for the remake of King Kong, things around him were taking shape. Abuja, for instance, was becoming the fastest-growing capital city (when other capital cities had stopped growing); Cecilia Ibru-him, the matron of clearinghouses, once again declared vast amounts of profit from the Ocean... which is not too far from derelict houses and residents crying for stipends to survive…

As I floated about the vortex, a marabout accosted me.

'What's going on…?' I asked the turban-wearing kaftan-clad hermit.

'Your country will be a great country'—

'Issalie', I cut him off.

'Issatrue!"

I pressed him to tell me when.

'Twenty-twenty…'. And before I could run my mouth he let open a portal and showed me the sign of things to come:

I saw Jack Gowon doing tricks for the British so as to get the hosting rights for the 2018 Commonwealth games, which has been ceded to Africa. The chaps were having a good time with this British-bred Nigerian pedigree. And then, one of the chaps I recognised as Tony Blair Witch, now the Commonwealth Secretary-General after rigging the elections in his favour, bent over to Jack, a stick in hand.

'Fetch!' he commanded, tossing the stick across the islands. And Jack did just that, zapping his way to Japan. By the time he's returned Banjul had the hosting rights, Jack had the stick….

'Awww,' Blair purred, 'you'll have it next time you want to mark one of those bland events of yours: centenary, bicentenary…you name it'. Meanwhile, the United States of Britain and North America, having been satisfied with ex-President Goodluck Jonathan's lack to response to incessant bomb attacks decorated him with the Nobel Peace Prize for Economics and made him Secretary-General of the United Nations. This was to ensure he kept a perfectly bovine look whilst his patrons invaded Iran to arrest Pope Khomeini III – the last obstacle to peace in the Middle East.

By the time I awoke it was 2020. I put my television (the same I used in 2007) and the Abuja Carnival was on. And by now it is now known as the Annual Harmattan* Cultural Parade. The NTA cameraman was busying himself with the hindquarters of one those raunchy dancers from the Calabar contingent. In the background, one or two embassy staffers with nothing else to do that day are snapping away pictures of some shabby vagrants with hi-power cameras that can zoom into several kilometres away. In the foreground the Culture Minster, arrayed in "Nigerian" attire (Hausa slippers, Yoruba cap, Igbo walking stick, Urobho waistcoat, Tiv sash, etc.) was been interviewed by a journalist who was anxious for the talkative to finish his ranting (the Calabar contingent was just filing past). The Minister was talking:

'As you can see for yourself Nigeria has become one of the largest economies just by exporting our women... and even as I'm speaking now, His Excellency the President Ben Murray-Bruce is already putting plans to make Nigeria the largest economy by 2050... '.

I relapsed into another dream....

---

* dry dusty weather akin to West Africa between November and April

Parting Shot

As a post-script the writer wishes to announce that he, she, it or they reserves or reserve the right to employ neologisms, phonetically alter standard linguistics units for effect, present partially distorted facts and endorse Nigerian parlance which defy logic (such as cousin-brother) .

Magode fe'ei

www.ingramcontent.com/pod-product-compliance
Ingram Content Group UK Ltd.
Pitfield, Milton Keynes, MK11 3LW, UK
UKHW041937190726
13854UKWH00004B/1631